CRISIS MANAGEMENT

CRISIS

Ian I. Mitroff

Christine M. Pearson

MANAGEMENT

A Diagnostic Guide for Improving Your Organization's Crisis-Preparedness

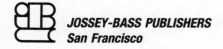

JOSSEY-BASS PUBLISHERS
San Francisco

Substantial discounts on bulk quantities of Jossey-Bass books are available to corporations, professional associations, and other organizations. For details and discount information, contact the special sales department at Jossey-Bass Inc., Publishers. (415) 433-1740; Fax (415) 433-0499.

For sales outside the United States, contact Maxwell Macmillan International Publishing Group, 866 Third Avenue, New York, New York 10022.

Manufactured in the United States of America

The paper used in this book is acid-free and meets the guidelines for permanence and durability of the Committee on Production Guidelines for Book Longevity of the Council on Library Resources.

Library of Congress Cataloging-in-Publication Data

Mitroff, Ian I.
    Crisis management : a diagnostic guide for improving your organization's crisis-preparedness / Ian I. Mitroff, Christine M. Pearson.
        p.   cm.—(The Jossey-Bass management series)
    Includes bibliographical references and index.
    ISBN 1-55542-563-1
    1. Crisis management.   I. Pearson, Christine M.   II. Title. III. Series.
HD49.M567   1993
658.4–dc20
                                                            93-16039
                                                            CIP

FIRST EDITION
PB Printing   10 9 8 7 6 5 4 3 2 1   Code 9356

To our families: Donna and Dana; Bryan, Jim, and John, with love and gratitude for providing the strength, wisdom, and humor to manage life's day-to-day crises.

Contents

List of Exhibits

Preface

Virtually no organization would go into business without significant insurance coverage, yet far too few organizations have systematic and integrated programs in crisis management (CM). This book is for those who are interested in correcting this state of affairs.

. . . .

A NEW TYPE OF THREAT

In the latter part of the twentieth century, a new type of crisis—human-induced or human-made—has emerged. For the first time in history, these crises have the potential to rival natural disasters in their scope and magnitude. Some pertinent examples are

- The release of deadly methylisocyanate gas from a Union Carbide pesticides plant in Bhopal, India, resulting in injuries to and deaths of thousands of employees and other victims living in immediate proximity to the plant.

- The explosion of the Chernobyl nuclear reactor, which spewed deadly radiation across all of Europe and caused numerous immediate deaths and unknown numbers of defects in future unborn generations.

- The explosion of the space shuttle *Challenger,* caused by the infamous O-ring, resulting in the loss of seven lives. In addition, NASA's failure to detect serious manufacturing defects in the Hubble space telescope compromised the effectiveness of a multibillion-dollar mission and demonstrated that flaws in an organization, if left uncorrected, can produce multiple crises.

- Threats of terrorism directed against a New York publisher for publishing *The Satanic Verses,* a book thought to be sacrilegious. This example shows that no business anywhere is exempt from potential crises, no matter how bizarre.

- The Exxon *Valdez*'s spilling of millions of gallons of oil in one of the most beautiful, fragile, and pristine parts of the world, causing untold harm to wildlife.

- The deaths of eight persons in the Chicago area, due to the placing of cyanide into Tylenol capsules. This crisis caused Johnson & Johnson to pull more than one hundred thousand bottles from shelves nationwide, at a cost of hundreds of millions of dollars.

- The nearly irreparable damage done to the reputation of Sears, a trusted institution, as the result of phony auto-repair charges. This crisis showed that actions designed to treat one crisis can set off an even worse crisis if managers do not understand the context in which the actions take place. (In the case of Sears, the bonus commission system for auto-service personnel that was established to offset falling revenues caused incalculable damage to the organization's most precious asset—its reputation.)

Every day, it seems, brings news of a new kind of human-made crisis.

THINKING ABOUT THE UNTHINKABLE

In today's world, it is no longer a question of whether a major crisis will strike any organization; it is only a matter of when, which type, and how. Depressing as this thought may be, there is no alternative but to prepare for crises, which are increasing, not decreasing. *Crisis*

Management is intended to help you overcome the psychological hurdle of "thinking about the unthinkable" by helping you anticipate and prepare for the worst. Indeed, the inability to anticipate crises is one of the major factors in their causation and escalation. The better you can anticipate every aspect of a crisis, the better you can handle one when it occurs.

There is no such thing as a preformulated crisis plan or procedure that can be pulled off the shelf. Institutions—their circumstances and their problems—are far too varied and complex to use a single universal plan or procedure, especially for the most critical problems. It is possible, however, to give you the necessary tools and techniques to formulate a set of crisis plans and procedures appropriate to your particular situation.

Since the field of CM is still in its infancy, it is vital that you understand something of the newly developing "theory" of CM. This "theory" is anything but academic, however—it is eminently practical. It takes the form of a framework that you can use to assess your crisis vulnerabilities and strengths. *Crisis Management* presents this framework and guides you in applying it to your own organizational context.

WHO SHOULD READ THIS BOOK?

Crisis Management is for those who have come to recognize and appreciate that the potential for large-scale crises of all kinds is inextricably woven into the fabric of modern civilization. The enormous complexity of the institutions and systems we have fashioned is one of the biggest contributing causes to modern, human-induced crises. This book is also for those who want to learn the latest tools and techniques of CM, so that they and their institutions can avoid as many crises as possible and improve their handling of those crises that still occur despite the best efforts and intentions.

Specifically, the book is addressed to senior executives, managers, and M.B.A. students. We have developed, tested, and used the material presented here with all three groups. Senior executives are especially important to the successful design, adoption, and implementation of an effective CM program: without buy-in and implementation by executives and managers throughout an organization, no program can succeed. Managers responsible for carrying out CM programs designed by senior executives also have a critical role to play.

BACKGROUND

We direct the University of Southern California's Center for Crisis Management (CCM). CCM was founded in 1986 to develop understanding of the causes of the broadest possible array of human-made crises. There are strong areas of overlap between human and natural disasters, but there are equally strong differences between them. Perhaps the most important difference is that, with very few exceptions, human-induced crises do not need to happen; effective management of human-induced crises is essential precisely because they are preventable. That is why the public is harsh in its condemnation of organizations such as Exxon and NASA, which should be able to prevent or contain crises.

Over the past six years, we and our associates—Judy Clair, Michael Finney, Mindy Kirby, Sarah Kovoor, Maria Nathan, and Thierry Pauchant—have interviewed more than five hundred people in over two hundred organizations representing virtually every kind of private and public industry. Many of those interviewed were the most senior executives in charge of CM, who held direct responsibility for crisis response and planning in their organizations. To better understand the role of CM throughout the hierarchy of organizations, we also interviewed middle managers, supervisors, and line workers. In addition to conducting onsite interviews, we have surveyed the most senior executives across multiple functions in the Fortune 1000 organizations. We have also conducted over a dozen crisis audits of public and private organizations. As a result, we have developed an understanding of the major factors that contribute to effective CM and crisis planning. Failure to attend to these factors accounts precisely for how and why organizations get into trouble. These factors, in effect, constitute a framework for assessing an organization's crisis strengths and weaknesses, as well as a model for improving crisis management.

In the course of our research, we have found that many organizations are *crisis-prone*. Such organizations are likely to get into or cause major crises in the first place and then to mismanage the additional crises that may result. Actions taken (or not taken) by these organizations often reflect the desire to deny their vulnerability. There is also a smaller set of *crisis-prepared* organizations, which, while not invulnerable to crises, continually learn how to reduce their chances of major crises and to manage more effectively those that still occur despite their best efforts. Crisis-prepared organizations not only act and think systemically but also take CM absolutely seriously. They consistently stress the importance of safety over profits. Crisis-prone organizations, by contrast, tend not to dedicate sufficient resources or attention to CM. They may have CM procedures, plans, and rules, but these are not implemented throughout these organizations. People working in such organizations know that, more often than not, the unspoken do's and don'ts of the culture value profits over employees, customers, quality, or the larger community. In such organizations, CM activities may be designed to fool everyone, but ultimately they fool no one at all.

ORGANIZATION OF THE BOOK

Crisis Management is organized into three major parts. Part One is a concise presentation of the general concepts that underlie CM. It is based on our own research and that of others. Part Two consists of a series of practical exercises designed to help you evaluate the crisis vulnerabilities and strengths of your organization. We strongly recommend that you have other members of your organization complete the exercises as well, since not everyone will agree on assessments and judgments. After completing the exercises, you will have a picture of the crisis-related strengths and weaknesses of your organization. You will be in a position to see clearly what needs improvement and to make concrete recommendations toward that end. Part Three presents a summary of components of an ideal CM program, so that you can compare your organization's CM program to the ideal.

A FINAL WORD

Crisis Management, above all, is a book about the critical-thinking skills needed for survival and prosperity in a complex global environment—a world more interconnected than ever before. In this sense, this book is about the new critical-thinking skills needed to do business in the new global economy.

Effective CM is complex, but it can be learned and mastered. Anyone who is open and willing can learn how to use the tools presented in this book.

Los Angeles, California   IAN I. MITROFF
June 1993   CHRISTINE M. PEARSON

The Authors

IAN I. MITROFF is Harold Quinton Distinguished Professor of Business Policy and director of the Center for Crisis Management, Graduate School of Business, University of Southern California. He received his B.S. degree (1961) in engineering physics, his M.S. degree (1963) in structural mechanics, and his Ph.D. degree (1967) in engineering science and philosophy of social science, all from the University of California, Berkeley.

Mitroff is a member of the American Association for the Advancement of Science, the Academy of Management, the American Psychological Association, the American Sociological Association, the Philosophy of Science Association, and the Institute for Management Science. He was president of the International Society for the Systems Sciences in 1992–1993.

Mitroff is author of thirteen books on business policy, corporate culture, managerial psychology and psychiatry, strategic planning, and philosophy and sociology of science. He has appeared on numerous radio and television programs, including "Financial News Network," "Window on Wall Street," and Michael Jackson's nationally syndicated KABC radio-talk show. His most recent books are *The Unreality Industry* (1989, with W. Bennis), *We're So Big and Powerful That Nothing Bad Can Happen to Us* (1990, with T. C. Pauchant), *Transforming the Crisis-Prone Organization* (1992, with T. C. Pauchant), and *The Unbounded Mind* (1993).

CHRISTINE M. PEARSON is associate director of the Center for Crisis Management at the University of Southern California. She received her B.A. degree (1973) from Queens College of the City University of New York in French and economics, her M.S. degree (1983) from California State University, Long Beach, in industrial psychology, and her Ph.D. degree (1988) from the University of Southern California in business.

Pearson's research focuses on the impact of organizational culture on crisis management and the human contribution to the cause and escalation of organizational crises, particularly in the petrochemical and service industries. She has published articles on these topics in *Industrial Crisis Quarterly, Academy of Management Executive,* and *Organization Science.*

As a consultant, Pearson has assisted in the implementation of long-term, systemwide change for a variety of public and private organizations, including American Honda, Chevron, First Interstate Bank, Red Cross, and the State of California. Much of the framework introduced in this book is based on her research collaboration with line workers, managers, and executives of Clorox, Dow Chemical, Kraft–General Foods, Mobil Oil, Occidental Petroleum, Taco Bell, and Transamerica Life Corporation.

PART

1

THE BASICS OF CRISIS MANAGEMENT

Four Principal Crisis Factors and the CM Process

C oncepts, tools, and frameworks are available to treat just about any crisis situation. Before we present them, let us begin with a brief case that contains many of the elements of any crisis, real or potential. After you read the case, turn to Exhibit 1.1 and jot down what you would do if you managed the company in question.

· ·

ABCO, INC.

Your company—ABCO, Inc.—is a large meat-packing plant in the Midwest, close to Middleton, a small town that provides most of the company's workforce. For years, ABCO has flushed waste products from its packing processes into a stream behind the plant. This has been a particularly successful year for the company, and processing volume has increased significantly. It has also been an unusually dry year, and the water level of the stream has dropped.

A recent editorial in the local newspaper described carcasses of household pets found near the stream and implied that animals drinking from the stream and fish in the stream are beginning to die in large numbers. With the prompting of the Concerned Citizens of Middleton, a state environmental agency tests

---

EXHIBIT 1.1   **Conceptual Tool.**

As an executive of ABCO, what would you do? (List and prioritize actions you would take and your reasons for taking them.)

1.

2.

3.

4.

5.

the water and reports that it is highly toxic because of waste contamination. Fingers are pointing to a variety of causes: your plant, stagnation, and insecticides from farming operations upstream. So far, all the dead fish and animals have been found downstream from your plant. Public outcry is mounting because the stream also empties into a small reservoir that supplies water to Middleton.

This morning's editorial claims that an unnamed environmental agency is in the process of issuing a warning: all water from the reservoir should be boiled before use because its toxicity is dangerously high. The warning allegedly states that it may even be hazardous to shower in the water. In the meantime, members of environmental groups, the Concerned Citizens of Middleton, and the town council have threatened your company with lawsuits that could force bankruptcy. They are demanding that you immediately stop dumping waste into the stream and that you take full responsibility for cleaning up all the contamination.

FOUR FUNDAMENTAL QUESTIONS

The most fundamental question in considering any real or potential crisis situation is "How can the crisis be treated in a logical and orderly manner?" In the next chapter, we will present a systematic framework applicable to any crisis situation. In this chapter, we will draw informally on that framework by summarizing how to analyze and respond systematically to a situation like ABCO's.

In our experience, most people jump right into the ABCO case, without stepping back first and analyzing it systematically. A more effective and straightforward way to isolate the key components of any crisis is to consider its four principal factors:

What is the crisis?

When did it begin?

Why has it occurred? (What are its *multiple causes?*)

Who is affected?

Behind each of these four main questions is a series of subquestions. Answering them is the key to analyzing the crisis.

What?

No crisis ever reveals all the information necessary to analyze it perfectly or completely. Critical assumptions must be made, and equally critical questions must be raised, at every step along the way. The first and most fundamental step is to analyze the crisis from at least two different perspectives: a *worst-case scenario* and a *best-case scenario*.

From the perspective of a worst-case scenario, we need to consider not only whether ABCO was at fault but also whether ABCO may have caused the crisis deliberately, through either action or inaction. For example, ABCO's executives have to consider whether one of ABCO's own employees may have caused the toxic spill through sabotage, or whether the spill may be the result of faulty maintenance procedures and schedules at ABCO. Responses to these questions trace the present crisis—toxic-waste contamination—back to possible earlier crises, such as those involving employee sabotage and safety issues.

No crisis occurs in isolation. A crisis is typically part of a chain reaction of other crises. Any crisis, handled improperly, can set off such a chain reaction. The worst-case analysis always asks whether the current crisis may have resulted from some other crisis of the company's own making. If so, what should be done now, given the likelihood that the company's role will be discovered? And what should be done if previous actions were clearly wrong?

From the perspective of the best-case scenario, what if ABCO is not to blame? What if the crisis was caused or fabricated by others? What if ABCO has a solid reputation as an industry leader in disposing of and treating hazardous waste? ABCO may actually hurt itself by engaging in actions that presume its guilt.

There is no way for you to know the answers to the questions in the ABCO case, because we have deliberately presented incomplete data. Likewise, in the early stages of a crisis, information is usually incomplete or faulty. As you work through any scenario, we recommend that you entertain both extremes side by side until one can safely be eliminated.

When?

The answer to this question is strongly influenced by the nature of the crisis. For instance, if ABCO's current crisis is the result of employee sabotage, and since virtually all crises send off early-warning signals, then the following series of questions should be considered: Did ABCO have any prior signs or signals of employee sabotage? When should these signals have alerted ABCO to its current crisis? Could sabotage be the result of poor employee morale? If so, when was employee morale last measured, and what were the results?

If ABCO is not responsible for the dumping of toxic wastes, then have there been any early-warning signals that other groups or organizations are out to implicate ABCO? Does ABCO have any damage-containment or damage-limitation mechanisms to prevent waste spillage from spreading uncontrollably? The importance of these questions cannot be overemphasized, for they are precisely the kinds of questions that the courts and the media will raise: When did you know you had a problem? What did you do about it? If you didn't know you had a problem, why didn't you? If you knew you had a problem but didn't do anything, why didn't you?

Why?

Virtually all crises are caused by simultaneous breakdown in interactions among technology, people, and organizations. Every organization has what is known as a core technology. The core technology of an organization is the primary technology involved in creating its key products or services. In service organizations, the core technology generally involves the transmission of information that supports the delivery of service. In an organization that manufactures products, the core technology is the operating and maintenance procedures that support the creation of its key products. In the event of an impending crisis, it is crucial to evaluate the status of the core technology. In ABCO's case, it would be important to determine whether filtering systems may have broken down, been sabotaged, been poorly maintained, been inappropriately designed, or whether all these factors exist.

The evaluation of technology must extend beyond auditing mechanical integrity. People, not machines, ultimately control and operate technology. All-too-human operators may handle equipment in ways not originally intended by its designers. Indeed, it is estimated that up to 80 percent of all accidents are due to human and organizational errors, not to mechanical breakdowns.

Unless we know specifically how people actually operate equipment, then any hypothetical risk assessments concerning probable failures of technology are useless. In ABCO's case, we might ask whether the operators may have neglected their responsibility by not changing filters when they should have. Did employees forget to close a critical valve? Could operators have overridden the warning signals and safety systems that might have provided an early warning of rising toxicity in the stream?

ABCO's own organization may also be at fault for not ordering regular inspection and maintenance. Operators and inspectors may not be evaluated or rewarded for preventing problems. And ABCO's culture may be at fault if it encourages an attitude of "If it ain't broke, don't fix it—ignore it."

Who?

The question of who is affected is equally important in analyzing the case and recommending actions. Which members of the organization may have helped cause the crisis or make it more likely? Which employees should be notified about this particular situation? Who ought to have detected the crisis before its full-blown eruption? Who, outside of ABCO, should be notified or involved in the resolution of the problem? Who should be on the team to handle this crisis and prevent others? These are a few of the "people" questions that must be considered.

ASKING CRITICAL QUESTIONS

Critical questions are at the heart of critical thinking. Such questions constitute the framework presented throughout this book. As a result, we are more interested in using the ABCO case as a vehicle to illustrate these questions than in answering them here. But we suggest that you take a moment and return to your notes on the case. To what extent did you assess the *what, when, why,* and *who* of the case? Did you miss important considerations (such as the origin, timing, rationale, or parties involved)? Did you identify assumptions in support of both the best- and the worst-case scenario?

Any effective crisis plan or procedure contains an explicit answer to each of the four main questions. Ideally, a good crisis plan or procedure specifies the following:

1. The range of prior crises that may have given rise to the current one, as well as the range of other crises that may result if the current one is not handled properly

2. Potential early-warning signs of the crisis, and the status of mechanisms that can prevent or contain it

3. Factors—technical, human, and organizational—that may cause crises

4. The parties who may affect or be affected by it

Most crisis plans or procedures are ineffective because they fail to spell out explicitly and systematically how to respond to each of these major concerns. Unless this is done, any crisis plan or procedure may cause more harm than good.

CRISIS TYPES

Potential crises and their variations are countless; no organization could ever hope to prepare for every possible kind of crisis. But the array of crises can be limited to a manageable set of *types*. Which types of crises should a particular organization prepare for, given its mission and its industry? Which types should be included in the crisis plans of every organization, no matter what the nature of its business? Which potential problems can safely be neglected? Are there clear criteria for differentiating between crises for which an organization must prepare and those it can neglect?

There are crisis "families" and prevention "families" that, taken together, offer the basis for an organization's crisis portfolio. To hedge an organization's risk, safeguard its crisis preparation, and minimize its crisis vulnerability, at least one crisis in each of the crisis families can be planned for, and at least one preventive action in each of the prevention families can be adopted.

Generic categories of crisis "families" range from technical and economic crises (such as extortion and copyright infringement) to human and social crises (such as terrorism and on-site product tampering). In interpreting different types of crises, it is important to consider these families as they may be applied specifically to any given industry or organization. Consider product tampering, which need not be limited to the traditional interpretations (injection of foreign substances into food or pharmaceutical products, for example). Interpretations can be expanded to include incidents in other industries (for example, electronic product tampering, as in the injection of false information into the *Encyclopedia Britannica*). By extending interpretations of types of crises, the organization expands its preparedness and reduces its vulnerability.

CRISIS PHASES

Regardless of the type of crisis, effective organizational crisis management (CM) involves managing the five distinct phases through which all crises pass: signal detection, preparation and prevention, damage containment, recovery, and learning.

The earliest phase, signal detection, includes the sensing of early-warning signals that, in advance of the crisis itself, announce its possibility or first occurrence. The *Challenger* disaster is an example of a situation in which early-warning signals were ignored. Indeed, after the event, a comprehensive trail of memos that were circulated at NASA beforehand was found. The memos foreshadowed the crisis. The difficulty, of course, is that organizations are bombarded with signals of all kinds. But organizations that are crisis-prepared make a deliberate point of probing and regularly scrutinizing operations and management structure for warning signals of potential crises.

The second phase, preparation and prevention, involves doing as much as possible both to avert crises and to prepare for those that do occur. Organizations that can be classified as crisis-prone exhibit a very different mindset from those that can be classified as crisis-prepared. Preparation and prevention in crisis-prepared organizations involve careful and continual probing of operations and management structures for potential "breaks" before they are too big to fix. In the Union Carbide chemical explosion at Bhopal, if the victims had only been made aware of a basic safety response—covering one's nose and mouth with wet rags to avoid inhaling methylisocyanate gas—many of them might have survived.

Damage containment is intended to keep a crisis from affecting uncontaminated parts of an organization or its environment. The environmental costs of the Exxon *Valdez* oil spill were intensified by poor damage containment (ineffective oil-skimming equipment) and ineffectual activities, during which time was lost in communications across divisions of Exxon. Damage containment is virtually impossible to *invent* in the heat of a crisis; as Exxon learned, not having systems and equipment in place can cost precious response time.

During the fourth phase, crisis-prepared organizations implement programs of short-term and long-term business recovery designed to help them resume normal business. These include identification of the basic services and procedures necessary to conduct minimal business, assignment of related business-resumption accountability, and designation of alternative operating sites. For example, First Interstate Bank was able to resume delivery of primary services immediately following a fire in its Los Angeles facilities because First Interstate maintained advanced computer backup systems and had planned thoroughly for availability and use of alternative work sites.

The last phase, learning, concerns examination of critical lessons learned form the organization's own experiences and from the experiences of other organizations. Many organizations do not conduct this phase because of the false notion that an examination of the past will only reopen old wounds. After a crisis or near-disaster, however, crisis-prepared organizations examine and contrast the factors that enabled them to perform well and those that inhibited their CM performance. As much as possible, they do so without assigning blame. Crisis-prone organizations, by contrast, place more emphasis on finding excuses and assigning blame than on learning.

CRISIS SYSTEMS

Examination of recent organizational crises reveal that they occur because of interactions between three systems: the *technological,* the *individual human,* and the *organizational/cultural.* To be comprehensive, crisis-risk assessments must include the analysis of management priorities for each of these systems and of interactions across all three. For example, unless an organization analyzes how individual human operators and managers will interact with technological systems, as well as how the limitations of "real people" will affect their behavior under stress and how organizational factors (such as reward systems and communication channels) will affect individual human response, risk assessments will be incomplete at best. Having analyzed the impact of such systems, the organization is then in a position to compare needs to capabilities, including available resources, facilities, and plans.

CM plans and procedures should detail such contingencies as roles and activities, lines of communication, membership on CM teams, and backup resources, facilities, and schedules. No less important than the formal, documented plans and procedures is the potential effect of the organization's informal culture on these plans and procedures. One of the distinguishing hallmarks of crisis-prone organizations is faultiness of their general mindset or belief structure. In interviewing executives, we have encountered far too many rationalizations for why organizations need not take CM seriously: "We're big enough to handle any crisis." "Accidents are just a cost of doing business." "Crisis management is a luxury that we can't afford." "If we have a major crisis, someone else will rescue us."

CRISIS STAKEHOLDERS

Many parties are affected by major crises. Stakeholders—that is, individuals, interest groups, and institutions who affect or are affected by a specific organization—represent the diversity of perceptions that an organization must consider in formulating its CM policies. In recent years, the set of relevant stakeholders has been expanded beyond employees, managers, and unions to include customers and even vendors. But effective CM requires even greater expansion of the set of stakeholders, to include parties even more removed from the organization: special-interest groups, local politicians, and competitors, for example.

There is another distinction between crisis-prone and crisis-prepared organizations that is related to the definition of stakeholders. Whereas the crisis-prone organization defines a crisis as something that happens primarily to it, the crisis-prepared organization looks at crises as they affect (or are affected by) not only the organization but also its full range of stakeholders. This difference is not trivial. It indicates a fundamentally different perception of organizational responsibilities and of the relationship between the organization and its surrounding environment. By the same token, we have observed that, even during normal operating circumstances, the crisis-prepared organization tends to monitor a much wider range of stakeholders than does the crisis-prone organization. Systematic examination of how a diverse set of stakeholders can affect an organization is essential to CM.

SUMMARY

No organization can prevent all crises, but, every organization can lower the odds of their occurrence, lower their costs, and lower potential crisis-related condemnation. CM strategies must do the following:

- Prepare for a broad range of crises *(what)*
- Attend to all five phases of CM *(when)*
- Consider cultural, human, organizational, and technical factors *(why)*
- Incorporate many diverse stakeholders *(who)*

CM performance depends on how well an organization assesses and manages all these variables.

Suboptimizing is not an option in CM. An organization cannot make up for poor performance in one area of CM by excellent performance in another. All the components of the CM framework must be considered, and their performance must be integrated.

Chapter 2 A Systematic Framework for Crisis Management

Studies of major, human-induced crises demonstrate repeatedly that four main factors or variables emerge as critical in their causes, as well as in their prevention: *types* of crises, *phases* of the crises, *systems,* and *stakeholders.* Each of these major factors in turn is composed of subfactors. It is essential to understand the role that each of these variables plays in order to create the most effective program of CM.

VARIABLES

In the last chapter, we introduced each of these factors and discussed them briefly. The purpose of this chapter is to consider them in more detail. In later chapters, we will show you how to assess the strengths and vulnerabilities of your own organization in light of each of these variables. Strengths and weaknesses reveal the crisis *capabilities* of an organization.

Types

Since the number of potential crises and variations seems endless, no organization, even with the best of budgets, could possibly prepare for all possible crises. What crises, if any, should your organization prepare for? In other words, what should be the *scope* of your organization's crisis plans? Should some kinds of crises automatically be included in your crisis plans, no matter what your business or mission? What crises, if any, can you safely neglect? Is there a clear criterion or rationale for deciding which crises to prepare for or neglect?

Phases

Do all crises move through certain generic phases over time? If so, what are those phases? What detailed activities does each phase involve? What has to be managed at each phase? Is it enough merely to react as a crisis hits, or does effective CM mean being proactive as well?

Systems

In virtually every crisis that has been studied, it has been found that the following subvariables played a critical role in its cause or origin: technological factors, organizational factors, human factors, cultural factors, and emotional factors. What are the subvariables, and how do they interact? What, if anything, differentiates between organizations that manage them well and those that do not? Are some organizations crisis-prone because they fail to give equal attention to these variables and to their interactions?

Stakeholders

Who are the parties (individuals, organizations, institutions) that may affect and be affected by your organization's crisis management? Can you anticipate and systematically analyze which stakeholders will be involved in any crisis?

INTEGRATED CRISIS MANAGEMENT

Figure 2.1 shows potential overlap and interactions among each of these major factors. (The main questions or concerns underlying each factor are summarized in Table 2.1.) The figure shows that every type of crisis

Figure 2.1.   **Four Major Variables in an Integrated CM Program.**

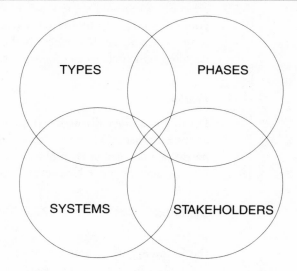

has to be managed across time, due to the fact that the factor phase is present in all crises. In addition, key stakeholders must be considered with respect to how they may affect or be affected by the interaction of technological, human, and organizational systems. In principle, every crisis involves a different mix of these factors. A systemic—that is, integrated—program of CM inspects how each of these different factors affects the total CM program. This is especially important, since a single crisis rarely occurs in isolation. For this reason, it is important that crisis plans and crisis procedures not be prepared in isolation from one another. A systematic inspection of organizational plans and procedures, and especially of the assumptions on which they are based, determines whether they may conflict with one another.

CRISIS TYPES

One of the first projects undertaken by the Center for Crisis Management concerned the determination of a typology of crises. Under the

TABLE 2.1.   **Major Questions Underlying the Components of a CM Program.**

- Types:
  Which crises should your organization prepare for?
  What should be the scope of your crisis plans?
  Which crises, if any, can your organization neglect safely?
  What is the rationale for including or excluding a crisis?
- Phases:
  What are the generic time phases through which all crises move?
  What are the detailed activities of each phase?
  What must be managed during each phase?
  What is the proper mode of response: reactive or proactive?
- Systems:
  Which variables cause crises? Which prevent them?
  Are the variables known?
  Which resources can be used to manage the variables?
    Technology
    Organizational infrastructure
    Human Factors
    Organizational Culture
    Emotions
- Stakeholders:
  Which stakeholders affect CM?
  Which stakeholders are affected by CM?
  How can you systematically analyze and anticipate the stakeholders for
    any crisis?

sponsorship of the National Association of Manufacturers (NAM), questionnaires were sent to the public affairs officers of the Fortune 1000 companies. Figures 2.2 and 2.3 illustrate the results of statistical interpretation of the nature of the crises experienced by the respondents' organizations over a three-year period. It was found that crises can be grouped statistically into major clusters, or families.

Figure 2.2 captures the underlying structure of crises, as revealed in the clusters themselves and in the two principal dimensions that underlie them. The vertical axis or dimension shows differentiation between crises that are perceived to be primarily technical or economic in origin and those that are primarily human or social in origin. The horizontal axis shows perceived normality versus the abnormality of a crisis. Crises located at the right of Figure 2.2 can be explained by relatively normal,

Figure 2.2.   **Crisis Families.**

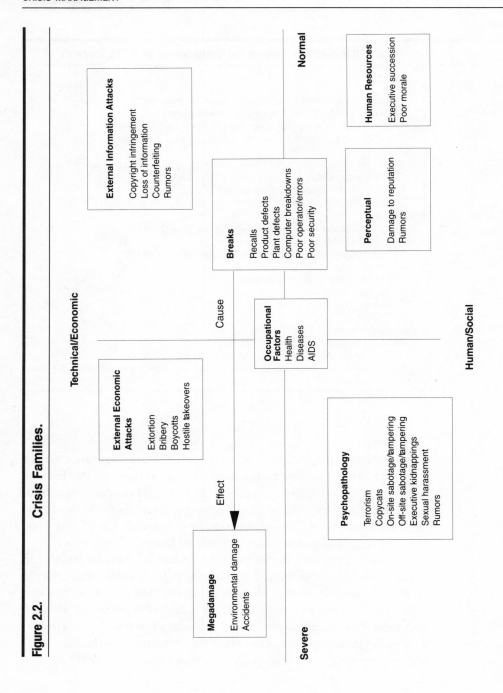

Figure 2.3. **Preventive-Action Families.**

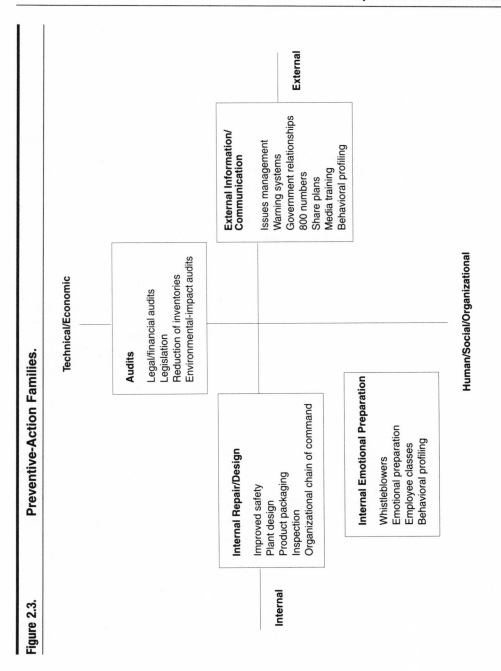

everyday events (such as the breakdown of equipment through normal wear and tear or operator error), whereas those that fall on the extreme left seem to have aberrant or deviant explanations or causes (for example, pathological explanations of human behavior, as in the case of a psychopathic saboteur).

As we have stressed, a single crisis almost never occurs in isolation. The simultaneous occurrence of multiple crises was more the rule than the exception in the NAM study. One crisis typically sets off a chain reaction of others unless an organization is explicitly prepared for this possibility. This suggests that every organization should prepare for at least one potential crisis in each of the crisis families shown in Figure 2.2, if every potential crisis in each of the families may be either the cause or the effect of any other crisis. It is generally too taxing to prepare for all of them. Since the various crisis families are distinct, however, preparation for at least one crisis in each of the families offers some degree of protection for each of the others in the same family.

The interpretation of Figure 2.3 is similar to that of Figure 2.2. Analysis of preventive actions reveals that they also tend to cluster into distinct families. The implication of both these findings is that every organization needs to form two crisis portfolios, similar in spirit and intent to a financial portfolio. To evenly spread the organization's risk and preparation, it seems prudent that at least one crisis in each of the families be planned for, and that at least one preventive action in each of the preventive-action families also be adopted.

It may do little good for an organization to prepare in depth for only one type of crisis, if a different type can render it just as vulnerable.

These recommendations carry a strong qualification: none of the items in any of the families must be taken too literally. Consider the crisis family labeled "Psychopathology" in Figure 2.2. It is tempting to interpret the particular crisis of tampering as simply meaning the injection of a foreign, poisonous substance into food or pharmaceutical products, but every organization can assume that an *applicable form* of tampering can occur within its own particular domain. What is the form of tampering that can happen to your organization?

The electronic distortion of information is as much an example of tampering as is the injection of foreign substances into food or pharmaceutical products. For example, the major French publisher Larousse had to recall 250,000 of its high-quality encyclopedias. At one point, two facing pages consisted of pictures of mushrooms that were safe to eat versus those that were dangerous. Apparently, something or someone had switched the critical set of labels distinguishing between edible and poisonous mushrooms.

Whether this crisis was due to product tampering or human error is not known, but the point remains: the specific forms that a crisis can assume are much more varied than the generic families themselves. New forms of specific crises are constantly emerging, while the general families themselves seem much more constant and enduring.

One of the ways an organization may get into trouble is by concentrating its resources solely on those narrowly defined crises that are endemic to or commonplace in its industry. While an organization must attend to crises that have historically been common to its industry, that alone is not a sufficient foundation for CM. The guideline in applying the variable types of crisis to your organization is to consider carefully how a *generic* type could be manifested in *your* environment. (In the next chapter, we will in more detail show how you can do this.)

· ·

CRISIS PHASES

Figure 2.4 shows the five time phases through which virtually all crises pass. With very few exceptions, all crises leave a repeated trail of early-warning signals. The difficulty, of course, is that all organizations, even under the best of circumstances, are constantly bombarded with signals

Figure 2.4.   **Five Phases of Crisis Management.**

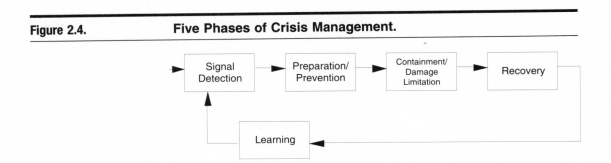

of all kinds. The challenge is in learning to separate the signals indicative of a looming crisis from the barrage of noise that is a result of day-to-day business in the information age. Even if an organization has a signal-detection mechanism, however, this may not be sufficient. A signal-detection mechanism designed for one specific type of crisis will not necessarily pick up early-warning signals for other types. For example, an auditing program designed to sense early-warning signs of technical defects will not warn of the potential dangers of slanderous jokes (which may be indicative of deteriorating morale or of a poor organizational culture).

Crisis-prepared organizations exhibit a very different mindset from those that are crisis-prone. Crisis-prepared organizations constantly scrutinize their operations and management structures, whereas crisis-prone organizations tend to miss or even ignore signals indicating potential weakness in operations or structures. In some cases, crisis-prone organizations even exert considerable effort to block warning signals.

Students and practitioners of CM generally agree that the *complete* prevention of all crises is not possible. The aim is to do as much as humanly possible to prevent crises and to do a better job of managing those that still occur.

Damage containment is precisely what its name implies. Its major aim is to stop the effects of a crisis (for example, by preventing a localized crisis from affecting uncontaminated parts of an organization or its environment). Damage-containment mechanisms and activities are virtually impossible to invent during the heat of a major crisis, which even a cursory inspection of such crises as the Exxon *Valdez* oil spill confirms. When appropriate procedures and mechanisms do not exist, or when organizational systems are in poor repair, the initial sparks of a crisis are soon fanned into full flame. In the case of the *Valdez*, Exxon's containment capabilities were significantly diminished by lack of appropriate skimming procedures and mechanisms and by ineffective communication channels.

The best-prepared organizations have programs of short-term and long-term business recovery. Recovery involves the following kinds of issues:

- Minimum procedures and operations that the organization needs to conduct business normally

- Critical activities and tasks that must be performed so that the most important customers and clients can be served

- Communication with most important customers and clients

- Designation of alternative sites for critical operations (such as computerized operations)

Insurance to replace computers may do little good. You can replace the machines but not necessarily the information stored in them, and all the insurance in the world cannot replace the business lost because of the loss of critical information.

The learning phase concerns reflection on the critical lessons that can be gleaned from a crisis, both your own and those of other organizations. Many organizations, having successfully managed a crisis, slip into a state of euphoria, believing that they now have the expertise to overcome any future crises. Other organizations, having barely survived a crisis, may find themselves too exhausted to devote their depleted energies to revisiting the crisis and sorting out the lessons to be learned. People may also be reluctant to "reopen old wounds." Crisis-prepared organizations carefully examine the factors that enabled them to perform well and those that did not—without blaming others. The emphasis in crisis-prepared organizations is on improving future CM capabilities and fixing current problems. We call this *no-fault learning.*

CRISIS SYSTEMS

Most organizations find it difficult to do well on all five system-related components of a crisis: technology, organizational infrastructure, human factors, organizational culture, and emotions. Many organizations focus on the technological causes of crises, without giving appropriate attention to the role of human factors and organizational (infrastructure or culture) variables. Even fewer organizations recognize how emotional factors contribute to major crises. For this reason, far too many risk assessments are limited to technical analyses of potentially dangerous situations. But unless you know how individual human operators and managers actually interact with technological systems, and how such systems are integrated in your organization, such risk assessment can be dangerously misleading.

It is also extremely dangerous to design technological devices or systems on the presumption that they will be operated by "ideal" humans. Designs must take account of the cognitive and emotional limitations of human beings, and of the ways in which people actually interact with equipment and systems. This is especially important in crisis planning: under stress (a major characteristic of all crises), human beings act neither normally nor rationally.

Effective CM requires an appropriate organizational infrastructure, including open and effective channels of communication between and across the various levels and divisions of the organization. Effective CM also requires the reward structure to support CM activities and the reporting of bad news. To be effective, the CM activities required of employees must be integrated with employees' ongoing activities, roles, and responsibilities. CM also involves the establishment of a permanent CM team, which represents all the specialties and necessary functions required to deal with a major crisis. Thus the president may sometimes, but not always, be on the team; as well as top managers of the legal, marketing, security and safety, environmental health, operations, public affairs, finance, and human resources functions. Members practice working together under conditions that simulate the informational and emotional overload they will face in a real crisis.

Equally important is the effect of an organization's culture on its crisis procedures and its vulnerability to a major crisis. Table 2.2 shows a partial list of the many rationalizations that are used to block CM priorities. One of the first indicators of a crisis-prone organization is its extensive use of such rationalizations.

CRISIS STAKEHOLDERS

Figures 2.5 and 2.6 show two ways of thinking about some of the stakeholders who may affect or be affected by a major crisis. For example, stakeholders may make a major crisis more or less likely to happen. In contrast to stockholders, stakeholders represent a much broader array

TABLE 2.2.		Rationalizations That Hinder Crisis Management.	
Properties of the Organization	*Properties of the Environment*	*Properties of Crises*	*Properties of Prior Crisis Management*
Our size will protect us.	If a major crisis happens, someone else will rescue us.	Most crises turn out not to be very important.	Crisis management is like an insurance policy: you only need buy so much.
Excellent, well-managed companies do not have crises.	The environment is benign (we can effectively buffer ourselves from the environment).	Each crisis is so unique that it is not possible to prepare for them.	In a crisis, we just need to refer to the emergency procedures we've laid out in our crisis manuals.
Our special location will protect us.		Crises are isolated.	
Certain crises only happen to others.	Nothing new has really occurred that warrants change.	Most crises resolve themselves; therefore, time is our best ally.	We are a team that will function well during a crisis.
Crisis management or crisis prevention is a luxury.	Crisis management is someone else's responsibility.	Most, if not all, crises have technical solutions.	Only executives need to be aware of our crisis plans. Why scare our employees or members of the community?
Employees who bring bad news deserve to be punished.	It's not a crisis if it doesn't happen to or hurt us.	It's enough to throw technical and financial "quick fixes" at a problem.	
Our employees are so dedicated that we can trust them without question.	Accidents are just a cost of doing business.	Crises are solely negative.	We are tough enough to react to a crisis in an objective and rational manner.
Desirable business ends justify the taking of high-risk means.		Crises do not require special procedures.	We know how to manipulate the media.
		It is enough to react to a crisis once it has happened.	The most important thing in crisis management is to protect the good image of the organization through public relations and advertising campaigns.
		Most crises are the fault of a single, bad individual; therefore, we don't need to reexamine and redo our management structure and culture.	The only important thing in crisis management is to make sure that our internal operations stay intact.

Figure 2.5. **Functional Organizational Stakeholders.**

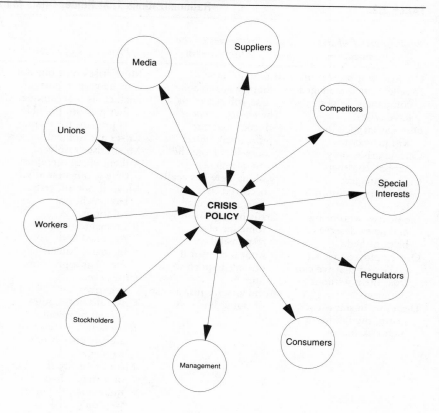

of individuals, interest groups, and institutions. In recent years, the number and diversity of stakeholders has grown rapidly.

The representation of stakeholders in Figure 2.5 reflects typical organizational functions: the internal members of the organization (workers, middle management, top management) and those external groups that may affect crisis capabilities (competitors, unions, the media). Figure 2.6 captures stakeholders according to archetypal roles or perceptions. From this perspective, the characterization of "villains" and "heroes" is especially interesting and important. A number of organiza-

Figure 2.6.   **Archetypal Organizational Roles.**

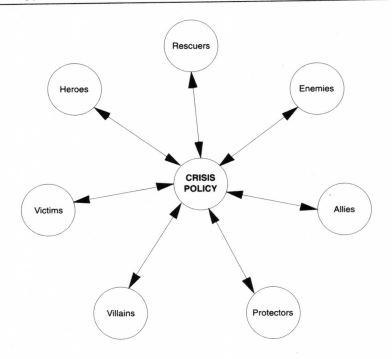

tions have recently discovered how easy it is to be cast in the role of villain. As a result, one of the most important things that any organization can do in formulating its crisis policies and procedures is to ask how it may be labeled or perceived by the outside world if it fails to act responsibly. Will certain actions be seen as characteristic of a villain? a hero? a victim? How can such characterizations facilitate or inhibit crisis containment or recovery?

The chapters that follow will help you assess the CM strengths and vulnerabilities of your organization. Each chapter contains diagnostic tools based on the CM framework we have presented in this chapter.

TOOLS FOR DIAGNOSING YOUR CRISIS-PREPAREDNESS

Chapter **3** Crisis Types

Determining Where You Are Prepared and Where You Are Vulnerable

*I*n today's environment, the total set of potential crises that could affect any organization is too large to prepare for, even with the best of budgets. To illustrate this point, Table 3.1 shows a "laundry list" of situations that could turn into full-blown crises. Obviously, this long list represents considerable difficulty in formulating strategies and dedicating resources, precisely because no one can predict which events or situations will or will not escalate into major crises. Indeed, in most organizations with which we have worked, at least one item in *each* of the alphabetical categories was associated with a major crisis experienced. This in itself shows the complexity and diverse nature of virtually all crises.

Like all other complex issues, CM is governed by significant uncertainty. Uncertainty does not justify doing nothing, however. Even though it is not possible to predict which of many incidents may become major crises, potential crises can still be grouped into families, or types, small enough to address. (See Figures 2.2 and 2.3.)

The diagnostic tools in this chapter will allow you to assess your organization's performance with respect to crisis types. To apply the framework to your own situation, we suggest not only that you use these tools but also that you ask members of other departments, functions, divisions, and job levels to use them as well. Since the assessment of an organization's crisis vulnerability is too complex and important to be entrusted to the perception of a single individual, regardless of how knowledgeable that person is, we urge you to see whether others identify the same vulnerabilities. The sharing of views about which crises your organization is prepared for and which possibilities it has neglected will provide a framework for identifying potential gaps in CM efforts. Discussion of why your organization has focused on certain possibilities and neglected others will also reveal key assumptions.

In Chapter Seven, we will discuss in more detail what the responses to the questions and exercises in this and later chapters are intended to indicate. For now, we will merely note that if the crises (or preventive actions) that your organization adopts fall primarily into one or two families, then this is cause for serious concern: your organization is not broadly prepared. Indeed, this is the first sign that your organization may be crisis-prone.

TABLE 3.1.   **Crisis Index.**

Abortion	Drug and chemical	Lying
Accidents	abuse	Mergers
Activist action	Embezzlement	Multiple-use issues
Acts of God	Employee injury	New-product failures
Adverse government	Equipment malfunction	New-product
action	Exposure	introduction
AIDS	Extortion	"Nightline"
Aircraft crashes	Falling reputation	No comment
Aircraft safety	False accusations	Noise
Airport safety	Falsification	Nuclear emissions
Airport security	Federal investigations	OSHA
Ambush interviews	Fiberglass	Political problems
Analyst presentations	Fire	Premature disclosure
Annual meetings	Foreclosure	Product recalls
Anonymous accusers	Government	Product tampering
Asbestos	intervention	Proxy contests
Bad debts	Government spending	Public testimony
Bankruptcy	cuts	Quote in context
Chapter 7	Grand-jury	Quote out of context
Chapter 11	investigations	Rationalization
Chemical abuse	Grass-roots	Reclamation
Chemical dependency	demonstrations	Rumors
Chemical spills	Hazardous-material	Sabotage
Civil unrest	accidents	Scandal
Competitive	Hostage taking	Security leaks
misinformation	Hostile takeovers	Seepage
Congressional testimony	Image distortion	Sexual addiction
Contamination	Inaccessibility	Shifts in value
Corporate campaigns	Inconsistency	"60 Minutes"
Corporate control	Indictment	Special-interest groups
Corporate governance	Insider activities	Strikes
Cost overruns	International accidents	Takeovers
Counterespionage	International	Tax shifts
Crashes	competition	Technology transfer
Customer misuse	International issues	Television interviews
Death (customer)	Irradiation	Terrorism
Death (employee)	Irritated reporters	Traffic
Death (key executive)	Judicial conduct	Transplants
Demographic changes	Labor problems	Transport accidents
Depositions	Landfill siting	"20/20"
Deregulation	Lawsuits	Uncontrolled exposure
Discrimination	Layoffs	Unethical behavior
Disparagement	Leaks	Vandalism
Divestiture	Leveraged buyouts	Visual pollution
Downsizing	Liquidation	Whistleblowers

Source: Reprinted with permission from the Lukaszewski Group.

EXHIBIT 3.1. **TYPES Diagnostic Tool: Overview.**

To begin thinking about the types of crises that could affect your organization, and the extent of damage that could be incurred, consider the following questions.

What are the three most serious potential crises that your organization could experience? Why?

1. _____

2. _____

3. _____

How well prepared would you and your organization be if these crises occurred *in isolation?*

What would you do if they occurred *simultaneously*—that is, if one set off a chain reaction that incited the other two:

EXHIBIT 3.2.	TYPES Diagnostic Tool: Crises.

Does your organization plan for:

		Yes	No
A.	**External economic attacks?**		
	Extortion	☐	☐
	Bribery	☐	☐
	Boycotts	☐	☐
	Hostile takeovers	☐	☐
B.	**External information attacks?**		
	Copyright infringement	☐	☐
	Loss of information	☐	☐
	Counterfeiting	☐	☐
	Damaging rumors	☐	☐
C.	**Breaks?**		
	Recalls	☐	☐
	Product defects	☐	☐
	Plant defects	☐	☐
	Computer breakdowns	☐	☐
	Poor operator/operator errors	☐	☐
	Poor security	☐	☐
D.	**Megadamage?**		
	Environmental damage	☐	☐
	Major accidents	☐	☐
E.	**Psychopathology?**		
	Terrorism	☐	☐
	Copycats	☐	☐
	On-site sabotage/tampering	☐	☐
	Off-site sabotage/tampering	☐	☐
	Executive kidnapping	☐	☐
	Sexual harassment	☐	☐
	Damaging rumors	☐	☐
F.	**Health factors?**		
	Occupational diseases	☐	☐

EXHIBIT 3.2. **TYPES Diagnostic Tool: Crises.** *(continued)*

G. **Perceptual factors?**
Damage to reputation
Rumors

H. **Human resource factors?**
Executive succession
Poor morale

Total number of *yes* and *no* answers

SOURCE: *Crisis Management,* by Ian I. Mitroff and Christine M. Pearson. San Franciso: Jossey-Bass Publishers, © 1993. Permission to reproduce and distribute material (with copyright notice visible) is hereby granted. If material is to be used in a for-profit compilation, please contact publisher for permission.

EXHIBIT 3.2.   **TYPES Diagnostic Tool: Crises.** *(continued)*

Scoring

How well prepared are you for a variety of crisis TYPES? Transfer your total *yes* score onto the response bar below. As you review your responses, consider these questions: Does your level of preparation reflect concentrated efforts for only one or two types of crises? Which areas remain vulnerable? Is there a conscious effort under way to develop a broader crisis portfolio that represents the full set of risks your organization faces?

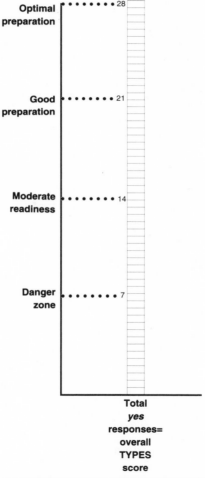

Optimal preparation •••••• 28

Good preparation •••••• 21

Moderate readiness •••••• 14

Danger zone •••••• 7

Total
yes
responses=
overall
TYPES
score

SOURCE: *Crisis Management,* by Ian I. Mitroff and Christine M. Pearson. San Franciso: Jossey-Bass Publishers, © 1993. Permission to reproduce and distribute material (with copyright notice visible) is hereby granted. If material is to be used in a for-profit compilation, please contact publisher for permission.

EXHIBIT 3.3. **TYPES Diagnostic Tool: Crisis-Preventive Actions.**

Has your organization adopted any of the following preventative actions?

		Yes	No
A.	**Strategic activities**		
	Corporate philosophy supports CM	☐	☐
	Integration of CM in statements and notions of corporate excellence	☐	☐
	Integration of CM in strategic planning processes	☐	☐
	Inclusion of outsiders on board, CM unit team	☐	☐
	Training and workshops in CM	☐	☐
	Crisis simulations	☐	☐
	Diversification and portfolio strategies for CM	☐	☐
	Section A subtotal	____	____
B.	**Technical and structural activities**		
	Creation of a CM unit or team	☐	☐
	Creation of dedicated budget for CM	☐	☐
	Continual development and changing of emergency policies and manuals	☐	☐
	Computerized inventories of plants' employees, products, and capabilities	☐	☐
	Creation of a strategic emergency room or facilities	☐	☐
	Reduction of hazardous products, services, and production processes (tamper-resistant packaging)	☐	☐
	Improved overall design and safety of product and production	☐	☐
	Technological redundancy (such as computer backup)	☐	☐
	Use of outside expert and services in CM	☐	☐
	Section B subtotal	____	____

EXHIBIT 3.3.   **TYPES Diagnostic Tool: Crisis-Preventive Actions.** *(continued)*

C.   **Evaluation and diagnostic activities**

Legal and financial audit of threats and liabilities ☐ ☐

Modifications in insurance coverage ☐ ☐

Environmental-impact audits ☐ ☐

Ranking of most critical activities necessary for
daily operations ☐ ☐

Early-warning signal detection, scanning, issues
management ☐ ☐

Dedicated research on potential hidden dangers ☐ ☐

Critical follow-up of past crises ☐ ☐

Stringent maintenance and inspection schedule ☐ ☐

Section C subtotal —— ——

D.   **Communication activities**

Media training for CM ☐ ☐

Major efforts in public relations ☐ ☐

Increased information to local communities ☐ ☐

Increased relationships with intervening
stakeholder groups (police, media) ☐ ☐

Increased collaboration or lobbying among
stakeholders ☐ ☐

Use of new communication technologies
and channels ☐ ☐

Dedicated phone numbers for recall and
consumers ☐ ☐

Section D subtotal —— ——

EXHIBIT 3.3. **TYPES Diagnostic Tool: Crisis-Preventive Actions.** *(continued)*

E. **Psychological and cultural activities**

Strong top management commitment to CM

Increased relationships with activist group

Improved acceptance of whistleblowers

Increased knowledge of criminal behavior

Increased visibility of the human and emotional
impacts of crises

Psychological support to employees

Stress management and management of anxiety

Symbolic recall and corporate memory of past
crises and dangers

Monitoring of cultural perceptions across
employee groups

Section E subtotal

Subtotal for sections A–E

EXHIBIT 3.3.	**TYPES Diagnostic Tool: Crisis-Preventive Actions.** *(continued)*

Scoring

How well prepared are you for a variety of crisis TYPES? Transfer your total *yes* score onto the response bar below. As you review your responses, consider these questions: Does your level of preparation reflect concentrated efforts for only one or two types of crises? Which areas remain vulnerable? Is there a conscious effort under way to develop a broader crisis portfolio that represents the full set of risks your organization faces?

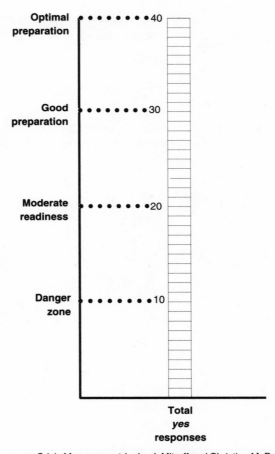

Total
yes
responses

SOURCE: *Crisis Management,* by Ian I. Mitroff and Christine M. Pearson. San Franciso: Jossey-Bass Publishers, © 1993. Permission to reproduce and distribute material (with copyright notice visible) is hereby granted. If material is to be used in a for-profit compilation, please contact publisher for permission.

EXHIBIT 3.4.   **Critical Questions for TYPES.**

1. How well prepared has your organization been for the crises it has experienced?

2. Which crises is your organization currently prepared for, and why? On Figure 2.2, indicate the crises for which your organization is prepared.

3. Which possible crises has your organization neglected, and why? On Figure 2.2, indicate the crises for which your organization is not prepared.

EXHIBIT 3.4.   **Critical Questions for TYPES.** *(continued)*

---

4. What key assumptions has your organization made about why it should focus on certain possible crises and neglect others?

5. Are your organization's assumptions still valid? Why?

6. Which additional crises should your organization prepare for? Why?

EXHIBIT 3.4.   **Critical Questions for TYPES.** *(continued)*

---

7.   Which preventive actions in Figure 2.3 has your organization adopted/ neglected?

8.   Is there a pattern in the preventive actions your organization has taken? For example, do your organization's efforts tend only to incorporate technical solutions?

EXHIBIT 3.4.	**Critical Questions for TYPES.** *(continued)*

9. Are there identifiable gaps in your organization's use of preventive actions? What critical vulnerabilities might these gaps expose?

10. In your organization, what are the biggest obstacles to preparing for a variety of potential crises?

11. Across your organization (comparing responses given by different individuals), are there systematic differences in the responses to questions 1 through 10? If so, what might these differences imply?

SOURCE: *Crisis Management,* by Ian I. Mitroff and Christine M. Pearson. San Franciso: Jossey-Bass Publishers, © 1993. Permission to reproduce and distribute material (with copyright notice visible) is hereby granted. If material is to be used in a for-profit compilation, please contact publisher for permission.

Chapter 4 Crisis Phases

Managing Across the Crisis Timeline, from Early Warning Through Recovery and Learning

In Chapter Two, we described the five phases through which all crises proceed (see Figure 2.4). As you review the figure, consider how well your organization is able to cope with each phase. Most organizations concentrate their resources and efforts on crisis containment and damage limitation. Some organizations dedicate time, equipment, and manpower to crisis preparation and planning for business recovery. But few organizations allocate substantial resources to detecting the warning signals of impending crises, and fewer still spend time and money on formally reviewing and integrating lessons learned from crisis or near-crisis experiences.

Figure 2.4 indicates that CM is a cyclical process. The actions you take to handle a current crisis affect your organization's ability to manage future crises. For this reason, we urge you to consider the full array of CM options, from detecting initial signals to documenting and incorporating the lessons learned (see Exhibit 4.1).

Exhibit 4.2 lists a variety of actions that can be taken to address the needs arising during each phase. As you evaluate your organization's crisis capabilities, think about the amount of attention given to each variable, the value and breadth of resources dedicated to each option, and the general attitude with respect to each issue. As before, we strongly recommend that you elicit the views of other members of your organization.

Exhibit 4.3 will help you gain a better understanding of how well the five phases are being managed in your organization. A cause for major concern is indicated when one or more phases receive attention at the expense of the others.

EXHIBIT 4.1. **PHASES Diagnostic Tool: Overview.**

In addressing the individual phases of CM, it is important to consider the following issues:

Do your organization's general crisis plans cover . . . ?

	Yes	No
the signal-detection phase?	☐	☐
the preparation/prevention phase?	☐	☐
the containment/damage-limitation phase?	☐	☐
the recovery phase?	☐	☐
the learning phase?	☐	☐
Total number of yes and no answers	___	___

Rank the extent to which your organization devotes resources to the various phases of CM (1 = most resources, 5 = least resources).

signal detection	___
preparation/prevention	___
containment/damage limitation	___
recovery	___
learning	___

EXHIBIT 4.2.   **PHASES Diagnostic Tool: Current Capability.**

Instructions: To get a general sense of how well your organization currently manages the phases of CM, mark your opinion about each of these items along the line to the right. For example, if your organization has signal-detection mechanisms (SDMs) that you rate moderately effective, your response will look like this:

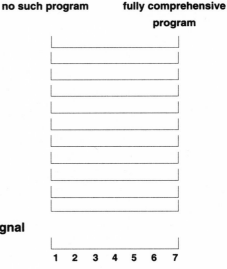

no such program   **fully comprehensive program**

Phase 1: Signal Detection
Signal-detection mechanisms (SDMs) for any crisis
SDMs for the most likely crises
SDMs for a broad range of crises
SDMs that build on existing data bases
Internal "assassin" team to test procedures
Recognition and rewards for people using SDMs
Formal job descriptions that include use of SDMs
Reporting structure that centers on CM
Central receiving point for detected signals
Compilation of statistics about crises and near-crises
Cultural support for signal detection
Please indicate the estimated average score for signal detection:

1   2   3   4   5   6   7

EXHIBIT 4.2. **PHASES Diagnostic Tool: Current Capability.** *(continued)*

Phase 2: Preparation/Prevention

no such program | fully comprehensive program

Mandatory probing for crises

Regular inspection and maintenance of all sites

Formal technical manuals and procedures using CM tools (hazard analysis, fault trees)

Human-factors analysis of critical equipment

Control of operators' workload to avoid excess

Management of system complexity, to avoid excess

Incorporation of organizational learning as system and technologies evolve

Please indicate the estimated average score for preparation/prevention:

1 2 3 4 5 6 7

Phase 3: Containment/Damage Limitation

could do much better | doing great job

Maintenance of containment information

Updating of containment capabilities

Testing of containment capabilities

Implementation of containment mechanisms

Recognition and rewards for damage containment

Assignment of accountability for damage containment

Please indicate the estimated average score for containment/damage limitation:

1 2 3 4 5 6 7

EXHIBIT 4.2.   **PHASES Diagnostic Tool: Current Capability.** *(continued)*

	could do much better		doing great job
Phase 4: Recovery			
Identification of stakeholders most important to recovery			
Identification of minimum tasks, services, products needed to maintain business			
Obtaining of resources needed to support minimum resumption			
Identification of on-site and off-site needs			
Identification of means of self-sufficiency if crisis causes isolation from rest of company			
Prioritizing of minimum needs			
Building in of redundancies most critical to business resumption			
Assessment of potential interactions of technological and human demands on recovery plans			
Please indicate the estimated average score for recovery:			

1 2 3 4 5 6 7

	could do much better		doing great job
Phase 5: Learning			
Review of crises or near-crises			
Review of crisis management, without blame			
Contrasting of things done well with things done poorly			
Generalization of learning to other potential crises			
Formal acknowledgment of lessons learned			
Brainstorming and creativity within CM review team			
Formal remembering and recognition of crisis anniversaries			
Please indicate the estimated average score for learning:			

1 2 3 4 5 6

EXHIBIT 4.2. **PHASES Diagnostic Tool: Current Capability.** *(continued)*

Scoring

Please transfer your average scores for each of the crisis phases onto the bars below. Once you have completed the average scores for each individual phase, use the last column on the right side of the page to estimate your overall PHASES average.

	Phase 1: Signal Detection	Phase 2: Preparation/ Prevention	Phase 3: Containment/ Damage Limitation	Phase 4: Recovery	Phase 5: Learning	Overall PHASES Average
Optimal Preparation	7	7	7	7	7	7
	6	6	6	6	6	6
Moderate Readiness	5	5	5	5	5	5
	4	4	4	4	4	4
Danger Zone	3	3	3	3	3	3
	2	2	2	2	2	2
		1	1	1	1	1

SOURCE: *Crisis Management*, by Ian I. Mitroff and Christine M. Pearson. San Francisco: Jossey-Bass Publishers, © 1993. Permission to reproduce and distribute material (with copyright notice visible) is hereby granted. If material is to be used in a for-profit compilation, please contact publisher for permission.

EXHIBIT 4.3. **Critical Questions for PHASES.**

---

1. Does your organization have a corporate vision for CM? What is it? Does it address the various phases?

2. Has the proper planning been done regarding who will be involved in each of the phases of CM?

3. List the actual capabilities that your organization has in each area, as well as plans to improve your organization's capabilities.

   Signal detection

   Preparation/prevention

   Containment/damage limitation

   Recovery

   Learning

EXHIBIT 4.3.   **Critical Questions for PHASES.** *(continued)*

4.   On which phase(s) are the majority of your organization's CM efforts concentrated?

5.   On which phase(s) is there a shortage of CM efforts?

6.   What kind of attention and rewards do people receive when they contribute to each of the phases?

7.   Are there phases for which employees' responsibilities and rewards could be increased or improved?

EXHIBIT 4.3.   **Critical Questions for PHASES.** *(continued)*

---

8.   How well does your organization plan for all five phases?

9.   What barriers keep people from planning for all five phases?

10.   How could these barriers be overcome?

SOURCE: *Crisis Management,* by Ian I. Mitroff and Christine M. Pearson. San Francisco: Jossey-Bass Publishers, © 1993. Permission to reproduce and distribute material (with copyright notice visible) is hereby granted. If material is to be used in a for-profit compilation, please contact publisher for permission.

Chapter 5 Crisis Systems

Assessing Your Organization's Technical, Organizational, and Human CM Capabilities

Technical systems neither exist nor operate in a vacuum. In most cases, the cause of a major crisis cannot be traced to the isolated breakdown of a technical system. Rather, crises occur because of the simultaneous breakdown of technical, organizational, and human systems. It makes no sense to analyze the systems comprising an organization's core technology in isolation from the human and organizational systems that implement the core technology.

Figure 5.1 presents an overview and a model of the systems variable, including the complex overlay or interactions among technical, organizational, and individual human factors that can both cause and prevent major crises. Figure 5.1 is constructed in the form of an "onion," to capture the constant interaction among all the layers that comprise the systems variable. Indeed, the intense interactions among subvariables contribute to the difficulty of trying to distinguish between and among the layers in actual practice. For the purpose of assessment, however, you will evaluate the layers as separate variables. Later in this chapter, you will be asked to consider the interactions among layers or subvariables.

On the surface, the technical aspects or technological operations of most organizations are the easiest ones to observe. In fact, these operations may be equally visible to outsiders and insiders. This is not to say that most people necessarily understand what they see, but rather that technology is often more visible than the other layers of systems. For

Figure 5.1.   **Layers of CM Systems.**

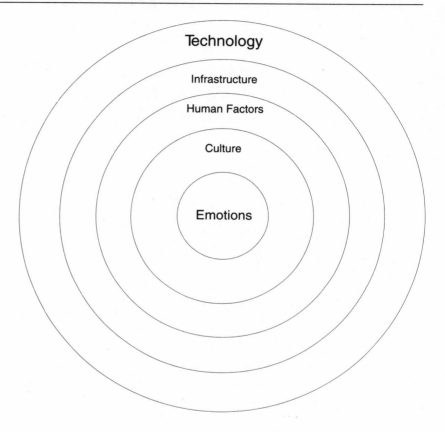

instance, you can *see* the technology involved in a chemical refinery merely by driving past it, even though you would need an engineering education to *understand* how the technology can be designed and safely managed. Technical aspects include the equipment and machinery that enable work to get done, as well as the processes needed to make a product or deliver a service.

One layer down, an organization's infrastructure encompasses its organizational chart, which depicts the formal power structure. Additional and less tangible variables, such as formal communication, rewards, and budget systems, are also components of the infrastructure system.

The components of the next layer, human factors, tend to be less visible. A specific example is the "mesh" or "fit" between operators and the machines they use.

With systems nearest to the core of the organization, a major difficulty is encountered in trying to observe or sample components. The culture of an organization is often invisible to, or taken for granted by, insiders and outsiders alike.

The innermost layer, the emotional structure of the organization, comprises the emotional responses shaped by senior executives. This layer is almost always unconscious, even to the members and the top executives themselves.

This chapter contains three exhibits that will help you evaluate your organization's performance on the systems variable. As we have emphasized, the process of discussing the evaluation, as much as the evaluation itself, facilitates the improvement of CM capabilities, especially when assessments are discussed by different people throughout the organization.

EXHIBIT 5.1.   **SYSTEMS Diagnostic Tool: Overview.**

Rank the following organizational goals (1 = most valued by your organization, 6 = least valued).

Profits   _____

Customer safety and satisfaction   _____

Employee safety and satisfaction   _____

Community/environmental safety   _____

Reputation   _____

Quality product/service   _____

1.   How well do your CM objectives and actions reflect this ranking? Are your organization's CM objectives and actions in tune with this ranking? Why or why not?

EXHIBIT 5.1.   **SYSTEMS Diagnostic Tool: Overview.** *(continued)*

2.   How does the culture of your organization aid CM?

3.   How does the culture of your organization hinder CM?

SOURCE: *Crisis Management,* by Ian I. Mitroff and Christine M. Pearson. San Francisco: Jossey-Bass Publishers, © 1993. Permission to reproduce and distribute material (with copyright notice visible) is hereby granted. If material is to be used in a for-profit compilation, please contact publisher for permission.

EXHIBIT 5.2.　　　　**SYSTEMS Diagnostic Tool: Layers of Crisis Capability.**

Instructions: Please describe your organization as a whole, by indicating your degree of agreement with the following statements, or by indicating other reactions, as appropriate.

A. Technical System　　　　strongly disagree　　　　strongly agree

Hazard and failure-mode analyses are performed for major equipment and facilities.

Technical checklists and manuals exist for major equipment and facilities.

Maintenance checks are performed regularly.

Major technical systems are integrated via systems engineering.

Risk analyses are updated regularly.

There are warning systems in place to alert operators that an error has occurred.

The warning systems are easy to recognize.

It is easy to differentiate among warning systems.

There are centralized command and control systems for critical technical systems.

Please indicate the estimated average score for technical system:

1　2　3　4　5　6　7

B. Infrastructure System　　　　strongly disagree　　　　strongly agree

Communication systems are integrated for CM.

Reward systems incorporate CM.

Business strategies incorporate CM.

Job descriptions incorporate CM accountability.

A crisis management team (CMT) exists.

Our CMT meets regularly.

Crisis simulations are performed regularly.

Our crisis plans involve workers at all levels.

We have stress training for CM.

1　2　3　4　5　6　7

EXHIBIT 5.2.   **SYSTEMS Diagnostic Tool: Layers of Crisis Capability.**
                        (continued)

We have emotional counseling for CM.

We reward people who report potentially bad news, even if they don't bring solutions.

We reward people who have good safety records.

We reward people who have good maintenance records.

We have a central receiving point for collecting information about crises and near-crises.

If a plant or division needs resources for safety reasons, they are provided.

Resources are available for analyzing plans to prevent failures.

Our organization has sufficient human resources to get the job done.

Please indicate the average score for infrastructure system:

    1   2   3   4   5   6   7

C. Human-Factors System   strongly disagree   strongly agree

Human-factors assessments are performed for major plants and departments.

Our control systems are inspected and designed for easy access and use by operators.

We track design faults or problems pointed out by our operators.

The amount of information an operator needs to operate key equipment is factored into design of key systems.

Physical requirements for effective operation of equipment are assessed.

Physical and emotional stress of using equipment is assessed.

The complexity of equipment and systems has not increased significantly in recent years.

    1   2   3   4   5   6   7

EXHIBIT 5.2. **SYSTEMS Diagnostic Tool: Layers of Crisis Capability.**
(continued)

Our training keeps people up to date on operating our
   newest equipment and systems.

Normal activities do not overload the ability of managers to
   handle information.

Normal activities do not overload the ability of operators to
   handle the tasks that they are required to perform.

There is formal accountability assigned for keeping
   procedures manuals up to date.

Procedures manuals are easy to understand.

There are shutdown or "kill" buttons for critical operations.

If work is computerized or automated, operators know how
   to bypass the system as necessary.

New workers receive adequate training before "soloing."

Please indicate the average score for human systems:

1   2   3   4   5   6   7

D. Culture System, Part I   strongly disagree   strongly agree

Safety practices are highly valued in our organization.

We do not value productivity more than safety.

There are opportunities for managers, engineers, and
   operators to discuss normal operating procedures.

There are opportunities for managers, engineers, and
   operators to discuss emergency operating procedures.

After an accident occurs, those who were involved are
   required to discuss "lessons learned."

There is an open line of communication between management and workers on safety concerns and errors.

The morale is good in this organization.

People in our organization actually get enough resources to
   do the job right the first time.

Employees understand communication that comes from the
   top levels.

1   2   3   4   5   6   7

EXHIBIT 5.2.   **SYSTEMS Diagnostic Tool: Layers of Crisis Capability.**
(continued)

People at the top of the organization get important information from lower levels.

People in different functional areas talk to each other.

People in different geographical areas talk to each other.

We keep our external stakeholders informed.

Our external stakeholders keep us informed.

Employees understand the values that drive this organization.

The values we practice day to day match the values we "talk."

People at the top set good examples for safety.

Please indicate the average score for culture system, part 1:

1   2   3   4   5   6   7

E. Culture System, Part 2   widely believed   not believed at all

The size of our organization will protect us from a major crisis.

Our special location will protect us.

Excellent, well-managed companies do not have crises.

Crises do not require special procedures.

It is enough to react to a crisis once it has happened.

Crisis management is a luxury.

Employees who bring bad news deserve to be punished.

Desirable business ends justify high-risk means.

Our employees are so dedicated that we can trust them, without question.

If a major crisis happens, someone else will rescue us.

Crisis management is someone else's responsibility.

The environment is benign.

Nothing new has occurred that warrants changing our procedures.

1   2   3   4   5   6   7

EXHIBIT 5.2.   **SYSTEMS Diagnostic Tool: Layers of Crisis Capability.**
(continued)

It's not a crisis if it doesn't happen to or hurt us. |_____|

Crime on the part of our employees is a cost of doing
business. |_____|

Most crises turn out not to be very important. |_____|

Each crisis is unique, so it is not possible to prepare for
crises. |_____|

Crises are solely negative in their impact. |_____|

Crises are isolated. |_____|

Most crises can be solved by technology. |_____|

It's enough to give technical and financial quick-fix attention
to problems. |_____|

Most crises resolve themselves. |_____|

Most crises are the fault of a single, bad individual. |_____|

CM is like insurance; you only need to buy so much. |_____|

In a crisis, we just need to refer to our CM manuals. |_____|

We are a team that will function well during a crisis. |_____|

Only top executives need to be aware of our CM plans. |_____|

The only important thing is to ensure that our internal
operations stay intact. |_____|

We are tough enough to react objectively and rationally. |_____|

We know how to manipulate the media. |_____|

**Please indicate the average score for culture system,
part 2.** |_____|

                                                  1 2 3 4 5 6 7

EXHIBIT 5.2.   **SYSTEMS Diagnostic Tool: Layers of Crisis Capability.**
(continued)

F. Emotion System   never   always

In this organization, people are allowed to express their
feelings.

No stigma is attached to the honest sharing and expression
of emotions.

No stigma is attached to seeking counseling or
psychological therapy for emotional problems.

People are aware that crises will produce emotional "fallout."

People are given preparation for the emotional and
traumatic aspect of crises.

Our employee assistance program provides emotional
counseling for crises.

After an organizational crisis or near-miss, people are
interviewed to assess the extent of psychological
impact.

After an organizational crisis or near-miss, those involved
receive emotional or trauma counseling.

Please indicate the average score for emotional system:

1   2   3   4   5   6   7

SOURCE: *Crisis Management,* by Ian I. Mitroff and Christine M. Pearson. San Francisco: Jossey-Bass Publishers, © 1993. Permission to reproduce and distribute material (with copyright notice visible) is hereby granted. If material is to be used in a for-profit compilation, please contact publisher for permission.

EXHIBIT 5.2.   **SYSTEMS Diagnostic Tool: Layers of Crisis Capability.**
(continued)

Scoring

Please transfer your average scores for each of the crisis systems onto the bars below.

Once you have completed the average scores for each individual system, use the last column on the right side of the page to estimate your overall SYSTEMS average.

	A. Technical System	B. Infrastructure System	C. Human-Factors System	D. Culture System, Part 1	E. Culture System, Part 2	F. Emotion System	Overall "SYSTEMS" Average
Optimal Preparation	7	7	7	7	7	7	7
	6	6	6	6	6	6	6
Moderate Readiness	5	5	5	5	5	5	5
	4	4	4	4	4	4	4
Danger Zone	3	3	3	3	3	3	3
	2	2	2	2	2	2	2
	1	1	1	1	1	1	1

SOURCE: *Crisis Management,* by Ian I. Mitroff and Christine M. Pearson. San Francisco: Jossey-Bass Publishers, © 1993. Permission to reproduce and distribute material (with copyright notice visible) is hereby granted. If material is to be used in a for-profit compilation, please contact publisher for permission.

EXHIBIT 5.3.   **Critical Questions for SYSTEMS.**

Technical System

1. What are the most common or frequent ways in which equipment has failed or nearly failed in the past?

2. What kinds of design changes can strengthen a particular technology or keep it from failing?

3. Is it possible to stop or reverse an error that might happen in your area?

Infrastructure System

4. Does the organization explicitly reward, rather than block, the reporting of potentially bad news?

EXHIBIT 5.3.   **Critical Questions for SYSTEMS.** *(continued)*

---

5. Do executives, managers, and supervisors unambiguously convey the importance of safety?

6. Do engineers, managers, operators, and safety professionals have any means of discussing normal operating procedures and emergency operating procedures?

7. Are there emergency procedures for dealing with the community? with families of employees?

Human-Factors System

8. Do operators' and designers' "models" or "mental pictures" of key technologies match? Are they significantly different from the formal, design models of engineering drawings or design specifications?

EXHIBIT 5.3.   **Critical Questions for SYSTEMS.** *(continued)*

9. How do operators and managers sense impending trouble, such as break-downs?

10. How do operators and managers cope with increases in equipment complexity?

11. What is currently done to ensure that your organization is a safe place to work? What more could or should be done?

Culture System

12. Does your organization have a credo or mission statement? What is it?

EXHIBIT 5.3. **Critical Questions for SYSTEMS.** *(continued)*

13. How highly is CM valued?

14. Does your organization conduct frequent surveys to measure employee morale? How is morale throughout your organization?

15. What are some of the most prevalent cultural beliefs that support or hinder effective CM?

Emotional System

16. To what extent do top executives believe that your organization is invulnerable to crises?

EXHIBIT 5.3.	**Critical Questions for SYSTEMS.** *(continued)*

17. How is the psychological impact of crises managed?

18. In the event of a crisis, are there plans for dealing with irrational behavior of employees or customers?

Systemic Interactions

19. How well are your CM efforts coordinated among the various systems?

20. Which of the systems are best prepared to prevent crises?

EXHIBIT 5.3.   **Critical Questions for SYSTEMS.** *(continued)*

21.   Which systems are most likely to exacerbate a crisis?

22.   How well are the systems integrated?
   a. Are safe operating procedures supported technically?
   b. Are there infrastructure systems that mandate and reward safety?
   c. Are human-factors systems analyzed, to maximize safe use of equipment?
   d. Does the culture support safe operations, even if that means added costs of time and resources?
   e. If a serious safety infraction results in a crisis, do witnesses receive emotional counseling?

Chapter 6 Crisis Stakeholders

Identifying the Key Players and Understanding Their Needs and Assumptions

The issue of how to anticipate and deal with various stakeholders requires more background than the other major crisis factors that we have discussed so far. For this reason, we present the following case study, which shows the importance of stakeholders, as well as one of the key concepts involved in critical thinking: how to bring key assumptions to the surface. A major crisis almost always calls into question or reverses the credibility of what was previously taken for granted about the behavior of those inside and outside an organization. For this reason, this section introduces tools for sharpening CM thinking about major stakeholders and about what is assumed to be true of them.

CRISIS IN A DRUG COMPANY

A large organization was faced with a problem that threatened, in one blow, to destroy its entire business. The company produced a painkiller that could be obtained only with a prescription because it had a narcotic base. A potential financial crisis loomed for the company. Annual sales of this drug generated millions of dollars, and growing preference for generic substitutes threatened to wipe out one of the company's mainstay products.

The CEO involved a dozen key executives, representing all the diverse aspects of the business, in the analysis of the problem: it affected everyone, and it involved aspects that he knew less about than others did.

The executives split into three factions, coalescing around the particular alternatives that individually made the most sense to them. Each group then proceeded to build the strongest case for its own alternative, to the exclusion of the other two options. The three alternatives were to lower the price of the drug, to raise the price, or to maintain the price and make cost-cutting changes within the company.

The first group wanted to compete head-on with the generic substitute by undermining the generic's price advantage. This group assumed that consumers are above all *price-sensitive*. Those who supported the alternative of raising the price argued that it was necessary to communicate to the marketplace the difference between the company's product and the generic. This group made an assumption about consumer psychology: people will equate higher price with greater *quality*. The first two groups were oriented toward the external marketplace. The third group focused on internal changes, arguing that if the price of the drug were maintained, then the company could raise profits by cutting internal costs. The third group proposed to do this by eliminating research and development (R&D), the largest source of internal costs. The argument was that if the current price of the drug generated enough revenue, and if the demand for the drug remained stable, then the company would not need to develop new products. This group recognized that, as a critical stakeholder, R&D would suffer, but the group also believed that the current crisis demanded tough action.

Each group had roughly equal power, and no group could force its alternative on the others. One group had to convince the two other groups, if the company was to embark on a course of action that everyone could embrace with confidence. How, then, did each of the groups try to persuade the others of the correctness of its policy?

The groups did what most managers have been trained to do: they analyzed past data (for example, past sales volume for various selling prices of the drug) and, where they could, they collected new data (from trade magazines and reports from field salespeople). The trouble was that, in this as in many other crises, the data did not settle anything. The figures actually made things worse, further convincing all the groups of the "truth" of their own assertions.

Besides holding fast to its own alternative, each group was assuming different things about the nature of the problem. Each group was taking certain things for granted, without conscious or explicit knowledge of doing so. Each group was also selectively interpreting the same data to suit its own particular case. In addition, where past data were not available, each group was collecting different data from different sources, chosen (largely unconsciously) to prove its respective case. Hence, instead of procuring data that genuinely tested each alternative, each alternative was directing its believers into procuring data that would confirm their own view.

The result was a circuitous process: decisions would have to be based on assumptions, as always in the management of critical problems; but since the critical assumptions had not been openly discussed or challenged, each group was a captive of its own stance. Management tried, unsuccessfully, to break out of this circle, using financial models and approaches to obtain neutral information that could clearly differentiate among the alternatives. But each group was making fundamentally different assumptions about the "real" nature of the problem. More data did not settle anything but only activated underlying differences. Since the assumptions remained buried, the groups themselves were largely unaware of what was happening; all they knew was that, time and again, they disagreed.

STAKEHOLDER ANALYSIS

What does all this have to do with assumptions and CM? Assumptions embody the presumed properties of stakeholders. In the drug company, the proponents of the different alternatives disagreed because they were assuming very different properties among the stakeholders' behaviors. In regard to CM, the bigger and more complex the crisis, the wider the array of stakeholder forces likely to be involved. As a result, more assumptions will have to be made. In impending crises, many important facts cannot be known prior to working through the crisis itself. Rather, a clear understanding of the nature of the crisis may only result from working through it.

In the drug case, the assumptions about physicians were the most critical assumptions being made, and these were the assumptions that were driving the groups apart.

75

The group that wanted to raise the price of the drug assumed that physicians would be motivated primarily by the traditional concerns of medical care (that is, concern for the health of the patient, regardless of cost). This group assumed that physicians were relatively *price-insensitive* and they they would prescribe a more expensive drug if convinced of its quality. A further assumption was that physicians' recommendations would overcome any countersuggestions of pharmacists.

The group that wanted to lower the price of the drug assumed that, because of the skyrocketing costs of medical care, physicians were becoming *price-sensitive:* they would no longer prescribe a more expensive drug merely because of its reputation; at some point, reputation would have to give way to economy.

The third group, which wanted to hold the price stable while reducing the costs of production, assumed that the marketplace was less pliable than the drug company itself was. This group believed that a strategy of reducing internal production costs would be more effective than one attempting to influence physicians' price sensitivity. Physicians were still key stakeholders, but not for their presumed cost sensitivity; rather, this group assumed that physicians were inflexible with regard to their preference for brand names.

Figure 6.1 shows an expanded stakeholder map of the drug company. Lines extend from each stakeholder to the organization and back again, depicting the organization as the entire set of relationships it has with its internal and external stakeholders. As these relationships change over time, the organization itself changes.

The failure to grasp this has prevented many organizations from seeing that they have changed along with the environment (that is, their internal and external stakeholders). Since we are dealing here with an organization as a system, a change in any one part potentially affects all other parts.

Every organization has some form of external competition, which affects the organization and its policies. In the drug company, it was the explicit threat from lower-priced generic competitors that initiated the crisis. But other stakeholders entered the equation as well. The company's sales force was an important stakeholder because whatever the company did would potentially affect commissions and hence motiva-

Figure 6.1. **An Expanded Stakeholder Map.**

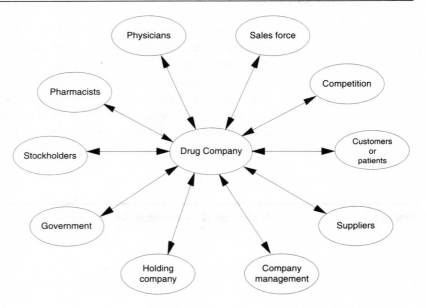

tion to sell the drug. Physicians and pharmacists were also important stakeholders because they had direct contact with patients, and their attitudes toward the company and its products would influence patients' behavior. Additional important stakeholders included the government and a holding company. The testing, release, distribution, and sale of drugs is regulated through the Food and Drug Administration. Because the drug had a narcotic base, the government was also a stakeholder in the procurement and regulation of raw opiates from foreign countries. The holding company was another, larger pharmaceuticals manufacturer that had a stake in whatever the subsidiary decided to do: if the drug company chose the wrong strategy, the profits of the parent company would surely be affected.

PLOTTING ASSUMPTIONS

Decisions faced in the management of crises always rest on assumptions of some kind. Assumptions can be displayed and examined in such a way that they can be openly debated. Figure 6.2 shows a map of assumptions in the case of the drug company. The importance of each assumption is reflected by its positioning along the least important–most important axis. People using this technique will feel more confident about the truth or certainty of certain assumptions, and this fact is reflected in the certain–uncertain axis. An assumption is most uncertain if it is as likely

Figure 6.2. **A Map of Stakeholder Assumptions.**

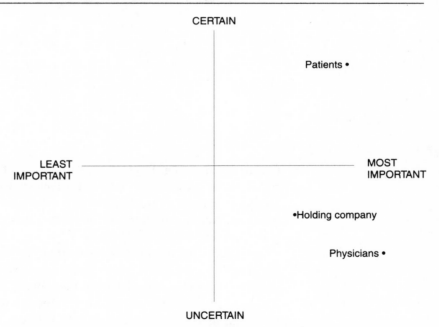

to be true as it is to be false. To use a common example, if the chances of rain are 50 percent (that is, the odds can be considered even regarding rainy or fair weather), then the assumption that it will rain is at the maximum level of uncertainty (and would be plotted accordingly, at the bottom of the certain–uncertain axis). If we know that it is already raining, then there is no uncertainty at all. Such an assumption would be positioned at the top of the certain–uncertain axis. Maximum certainty occurs when we have no doubt about the complete truth or the complete falsity of an assumption. Maximum uncertainty occurs when we have complete doubt about the truth or the falsity of an assumption.

All three groups regarded their assumptions about physicians as the most important and the most uncertain. Thus, for the high-price group, the assumption that physicians are price-insensitive was both the most important and the most uncertain assumption. Without the assumption of price-insensitivity, this group's alternative was not viable. At the same time, this group also held the most doubt about that assumption: Were all physicians price-insensitive? Did their price-insensitivity extend to all drugs? Or did physicians differ when it came to prescribing narcotics?

The second most important and uncertain assumption involved the holding company. If the recommendation was made to raise the price, then it had to be assumed that the holding company was primarily interested in maximizing profits. If the drug company lowered the price, as the low-price group was suggesting, then the holding company had to be assumed to be interested primarily in maximizing its market share. Neither perspective was wrong; which one was best would depend on the overall objectives of the parent company, the buying practices of consumers, and the needs of the subsidiary drug company, considered as a total system. Early decisions started with just one part of the system—the drug company—but additional components eventually had to be considered. This is also one of the prime features of crises: they essentially involve problems that affect a whole system.

In this case, the executives finally agreed on an alternative. They decided to raise the price of the drug in key locations and to monitor the reactions of critical stakeholders, thereby testing the truth of their key assumptions. If the price of the drug had been lowered when it could have been raised, then this action would have precluded any opportunity to find that out. If the price were raised in certain test locations, the executives would find out very quickly if the market would tolerate this action.

. . . .

DISCUSSION

The listing of stakeholders is a concrete way of getting at assumptions. Once stakeholders are identified, it is relatively easy to ascertain what must be assumed to be "true" about their behavior. Thus, starting from assumptions, decision makers can support their chosen policies or actions.

Far too many CM planning activities result in frustration or inaction because decision makers are unable to observe their own assumptions about key stakeholders. Mapping initial assumptions helps decision makers see their differences: about which stakeholders are involved, should be considered, and have the right to be recognized; about what the stakeholders are presumed to be like; and about what is important and what is believed to be known.

Too much is riding on any crisis situation for it to be pursued from only one perspective. As you think about the individuals, groups, and organizations that affect and are affected by your organization, consider what your organization takes for granted about their behavior. If these assumptions are inaccurate, how might they be keeping your organization from achieving its CM objectives? The following three exhibits will help you see how your organization deals with the variable of stakeholders.

EXHIBIT 6.1. **STAKEHOLDERS Diagnostic Tool: Overview.**

---

1. List the five most important stakeholders for your organization.

    1.

    2.

    3.

    4.

    5.

2. List the roles that each of the five stakeholders will play in the event of a crisis (for example, villain or rescuer).

    1.

    2.

    3.

    4.

    5.

3.   What has your organization done to ensure that your five most important stakeholders will act in the best possible way if your organization experiences a crisis?

4.   What additional actions could your organization take with respect to these stakeholders, to ensure their compliance or assistance during a crisis?

EXHIBIT 6.2.   **STAKEHOLDERS Diagnostic Tool: Current Array.**

Which of these stakeholders are considered in your organization's CM plans? Place a check mark beside the categories that apply.

Customers

Competitiors

Special-interest groups

Regulators

Top management

Middle management

Workers

Union(s)

The media

Consultants

Board of directors

Total

Which of these stakeholders take part in the formulation of your CM plans?

CEO

CFO

Chief legal counsel

Head of public relations

Head of security

Head of human resources

Head of operations

Head of marketing

Head of safety/environmental affairs

Representative middle managers

Representative workers

Total

SOURCE: *Crisis Management*, by Ian I. Mitroff and Christine M. Pearson. San Francisco: Jossey-Bass Publishers, © 1993. Permission to reproduce and distribute material (with copyright notice visible) is hereby granted. If material is to be used in a for-profit compilation, please contact publisher for permission.

EXHIBIT 6.2. **STAKEHOLDERS Diagnostic Tool: Current Array.** *(continued)*

Scoring

Transfer your total *Yes* scores onto the bars below. Use the last column on the right side of the page to estimate your overall STAKEHOLDERS average.

	Stakeholders Considered	CM Plan Participants	Overall STAKEHOLDERS Average
Optimal Preparedness	11	11	7
	10	10	
Good Readiness	9	9	6
	8	8	5
	7	7	
Moderate Readiness	6	6	4
	5	5	3
	4	4	
Danger Zone	3	3	2
	2	2	
	1	1	1

EXHIBIT 6.3.   **Critical Questions for STAKEHOLDERS.**

    1.   If a crisis occurs in your organization, who might its victims be?

    2.   Who would you expect to come to the aid of your organization in the event of a crisis, and what kinds of aid would these stakeholders provide?

    3.   Are there stakeholders who would probably block your ability to manage a crisis? Who would they be?

4. What actions are you taking to make it less likely that these parties would block your recovery?

5. What would you assume to be the response of people inside your organization if a crisis occurred for which the organization was not at fault?

6. How would responses differ if your organization were clearly to blame?

7.   How do you incorporate CM perspectives and CM lessons learned by others outside your organization?

8.   With respect to CM issues, which stakeholders' assumptions can be tested, and how might you go about doing this?

9.   Who are the most important champions of CM within your organization?

10. Who are the internal enemies of CM?

11. Who are the most important external champions of CM?

12. Who are the external enemies of CM?

Chapter 7 Charting Your Organization's Crisis Profile

*O*nce you have assessed how well your organization is performing on each of the four major variables—types, phases, systems, and stakeholders—you are ready to plot a *crisis profile,* which shows your view of your organization's total crisis-preparedness and vulnerability. To do this, go back to Chapters three through six and review your overall average scores. Then turn to Exhibit 7.1. To plot your organization's profile, mark each of the averages on the appropriate line, as shown in Exhibit 7.2. Next, connect the ends of the lines, as shown in Exhibit 7.2.

A crisis profile is a quick and easy way to see where your organization is strong and where it is weak. Any factor falling into the optimal and good preparation zones represents an area of CM strength; factors falling into the moderate readiness and danger zones represent areas of CM concern.

All the factors are important, but the systems variable is most important, and even more critical is the *culture component* of this variable. Difficult as it may be to improve crisis plans and install warning devices and damage-containment systems, an appropriate culture for CM is even more difficult to maintain, and changing a dysfunctional culture is the greatest challenge of all. If your systems rating is driven by a culture-component rating in the question-mark or danger zones, then you have real cause for concern. Any profile that dips into the danger zone on the systems variable represents extreme danger. Indeed, this is the strongest signal that your organization is crisis-prone.

Once you have determined your organization's crisis profile, you are able to assess its strengths and weaknesses systematically. You can see the areas that need improvement. You are also ready to consider your organization's crisis-preparedness in terms of the various stages of crisis-preparedness observed in many organizations.

Exhibit 7.1. **Crisis Management Profile.**

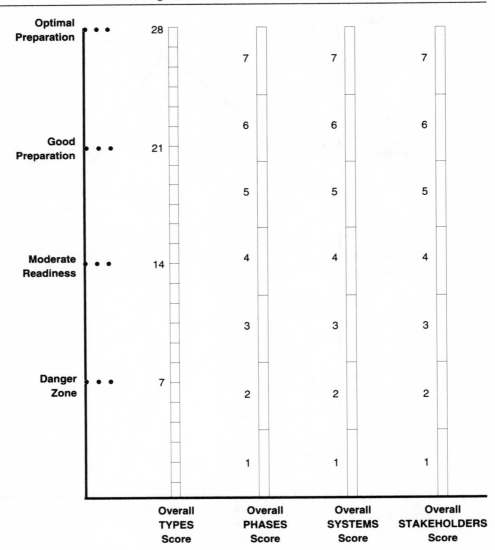

SOURCE: *Crisis Management,* by Ian I. Mitroff and Christine M. Pearson. San Francisco: Jossey-Bass Publishers, © 1993. Permission to reproduce and distribute material (with copyright notice visible) is hereby granted. If material is to be used in a for-profit compilation, please contact publisher for permission.

Exhibit 7.2.   **Sample Crisis Management Profile.**

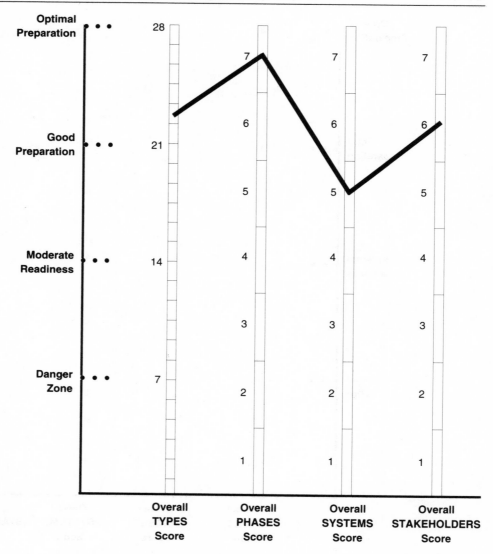

SHAPING YOUR CRISIS MANAGEMENT PROGRAM

Chapter **8** *The Five Stages of*
Crisis-Preparedness

T he five stages of crisis preparedness are easily distinguished in terms of organizational performance on each of the four major variables. In general, each subsequent stage incorporates the CM capabilities of previous stages, as well as additional CM strengths.

....

STAGE ONE

Stage One encompasses the lowest level of CM preparation, if indeed this stage can be said to involve preparation at all. CM preparations of Stage One organizations are typically confined to traditional fire and security precautions, although even efforts in these two areas are likely to be minimal. The procedures of Stage One organizations are likely to be implemented in a haphazard way, fragmented throughout the organization, and out of date.

The level of employee training with respect to what to do in a fire or other emergency is generally very low. In some cases, although plans may exist, employees in Stage One organizations are unfamiliar with their roles in implementing them. Few drills, practice sessions, or simulations are conducted, and the professionalism and training of those who hold primary responsibility in the event of a fire or other emergency are typically quite low.

Stage One organizations tend to deny their CM vulnerabilities. They limit their crisis preparations to situations for which plans are generic and readily available. Implementation of plans that address normal emergencies requires little commitment or effort on the part of the whole organization. Thus Stage One organizations are extremely limited in the types of crises they recognize and prepare for.

Stage One organizations are reactive. They have virtually no early-warning systems in place for detecting major crises, and few if any prevention programs exist. Planning for damage containment rarely occurs before the crisis hits, and recovery systems have not been established. Stage One organizations do not learn from their past mistakes because they do not conduct formal review sessions.

Stage One organizations have virtually no organizational infrastructure for CM, such as a dedicated budget or a crisis team. They may use many of the denial mechanisms described in Chapter Two, but they are rarely aware of their CM blindness. They often view CM as an expense that cannot be justified. Indeed, one rationalization often used by Stage One organizations is "CM is a luxury we can't afford."

With respect to stakeholders, Stage One organizations analyze neither how these key individuals, groups, and organizations are likely to affect normal business operations and objectives nor how stakeholders themselves are likely to be affected by or affect a major crisis. For organizations at Stage One, CM concerns rarely extend beyond their own employees.

At Stage One, it is also very likely that, if CM is championed at all, it is championed by a single individual. This champion is often in a middle-level staff position. He or she may be sensitive to CM because of his or her educational background or experience in another organization. At this early stage of preparedness, CM tends not to be a high priority for anyone at the most senior executive level.

STAGE TWO

Stage Two organizations represent a decisive advance beyond Stage One organizations. The Stage Two organization is much more likely to have a comprehensive program for responding to natural and human-caused disasters of all kinds (earthquakes, tornadoes, bomb threats, explosions, fires, toxic spills). Like Stage One organizations, however, those at Stage Two are just as likely not to plan or prepare for crises other than natural or human-caused disasters. The only exceptions are crises like sabotage or terrorism, which fall under the traditional heading of "security."

The Stage Two organization often has a dedicated budget and a structure for CM (although, as we have noted, it is limited to traditional security and emergency functions). Although Stage Two organizations are much more likely to have damage-containment and business-recovery mechanisms and procedures, they are mainly limited to those losses due to human-caused and natural disasters. They typically do not plan for economic attacks, such as extortion, or information leaks, such as copyright infringement.

Stage Two organizations concentrate almost exclusively on technical factors. As a result, they tend to ignore how organizational culture may make crises of all kinds much more likely. Generally, they believe that there are virtually no problems, in and of themselves, that cannot be cured through the development and utilization of more technology.

Stage Two organizations do not analyze how a variety of stakeholders may cause or be affected by major crises; CM plans and efforts still focus on stakeholders within the organization. A significant advance is made, however, from Stage One to Stage Two: interest in CM generally has spread to a few members of the executive team in the Stage Two organization.

STAGE THREE

The Stage Three organization is likely to have in-depth plans and procedures for a very limited number of human-induced crises that are highly specific to its particular plants, businesses, or industry. Thus, for instance, food and pharmaceuticals companies at Stage Three are likely to have detailed plans and procedures for handling major incidents of product tampering and product withdrawal. At Stage Three, such plans typically cover who is to be notified (for example, public affairs and medical personnel) and what is to be done in the event of certain circumstances (for example, particular types of food poisoning and contamination). The crisis plans and procedures of a company at Stage Three are likely to be part of a much larger effort, such as quality assurance (QA). The shortcoming for Stage Three organizations is that QA crisis procedures are highly unlikely to be integrated with other crisis procedures, such as those for extortion or loss of confidential information. Because of this fragmentation, Stage Three organizations miss opportunities to build deeper understanding of these crises.

Crisis plans and procedures of a Stage Three organization are also unlikely to be integrated at the division or corporate levels. Each separate division tends to have its own distinct crisis plans and procedures; little thought is given to the ways in which a crisis can jump across divisions to affect the entire organization. Another opportunity is missed because lessons learned at the division level are not shared for the benefit of the organization as a whole.

Stage Three organizations are likely to justify their actions with such rationalizations as "Only certain known types of crises are likely to affect us" or "Our special location or particular industry precludes us from having to prepare for certain types of crises, such as terrorism."

Stage Three organizations have begun to consider the impact of crises on external stakeholders. These individuals, groups, and organizations do not take part in formulating CM plans for Stage Three organizations, but key external stakeholders may be included in contact lists or be designated as recipients of CM information. Many members of the senior executive team may have begun to realize the value of CM.

STAGE FOUR

Stage Four organizations are much more likely to have integrated separate plans between divisions, and even across the organization as a whole. In fact, this is the major difference between Stage Three and Stage Four organizations. While Stage Four organizations are much more likely to integrate various plans across divisions and corporate headquarters, however, their plans and procedures will still be confined to relatively few crises, mostly specific to or endemic in the particular industries.

At this stage, CM efforts may be formalized for the earlier and latter phases of crises. In addition to planning for the containment phase, some planning may take place for crisis prevention and recovery.

At Stage Four, stakeholders outside the organization who are critical to CM efforts have been identified. From an internal perspective, the buy-in needed at the most senior levels is well under way. The original sole champion of CM no longer needs to exert pressure; in some cases, this individual may even be bypassed as senior executives set out to revise or enhance CM plans. Another typical characteristic of the Stage Four organization is the creation of a CM team, which will bear responsibility for facilitating and formalizing CM efforts.

STAGE FIVE

It is only at Stage Five that an organization approaches true crisis-preparedness. Stage Five organizations demonstrate strong CM capabilities, but this does not mean that they see themselves as immune or invulnerable to crises. Indeed, such organizations are much more likely to be aware of how vulnerable they are.

Stage Five organizations plan and prepare for at least one crisis in each of the crisis "families." They are also much more likely to have adopted at least one preventive action in each of the preventive "families." Stage Five organizations are much more likely to attend to each of the phases of CM. They have early-warning signal detection, engage in preparation and probing actions and procedures, design and implement damage-containment mechanisms far in advance of actual crises, invest in and implement business-recovery mechanisms, and incorporate learning without unduly assigning blame (unless specific stakeholders have been found directly culpable).

Stage Five organizations are likely to develop plans and procedures that explicitly take into account all the critical systems that enter into causing and preventing major crises. They do not see the causes of crises as purely technical; they are sensitive to human, organizational, and emotional factors as well. As a result, they are much more likely to have explicit programs that address human-factors issues (such as cognitive and informational demands of critical jobs). These crisis-prepared organizations have a greater awareness of the underlying organizational culture and how it contributes, positively as well as negatively, to CM. They are also much more likely to conduct formal analysis of issues and stakeholders. In conducting such analyses, Stage Five organizations raise their concern for a broad set of stakeholders to the public level. They may even take actions to fold this wider range of stakeholders into their CM efforts. Board members and line workers may be represented on the CM team; and vendors may take part in CM simulations. Stage Five organizations may share their CM experiences and expertise across their industries, even with competitors.

The progress needed to reach Stage Five cannot be attained without the commitment of the entire organization. At Stage Five, CM is not simply a nice philosophy; it is a value in action. The organization's buy-in is carried out through role modeling, resource allocation, performance accountability, and reward systems. Furthermore, at Stage Five, these actions and resources support CM efforts across all types of crises.

Chapter **9**

What to Do During a Crisis

Putting the CM Process Model to Work

We have found repeatedly that even an organization that values CM often concentrates its resources and efforts on managing a crisis *while it occurs*. The CM literature also focuses on strategies applicable during a crisis. But there is much more to be gained by expanding CM efforts to incorporate practical actions to be taken both before and after a crisis. Nevertheless, we do recognize the need for action during a crisis.

In the heat of a crisis, a number of the activities must be performed simultaneously, which means that these activities will overlap. During the first few hours (and throughout the first week or even longer), the critical responsibilities of crisis managers will be fact finding, analysis, damage control, and communication.

· ·

FACT FINDING

The fact-finding period has the immediate goal of assessing damage. How much damage has been done to the environment? How much damage has been done to business facilities?

ANALYSIS

It is necessary to uncover the cause of the crisis. Was the crisis due to a breakdown in the organization's core manufacturing or production technologies? Was it caused by faulty maintenance or processing technologies, or by misinformation? Was the crisis due primarily to human error? What role, if any, did human factors play? Did the organization's infrastructure contribute to the crisis through a breakdown in communication, roles, authority, or reward structures? How did the organization's culture contribute to causing or containing the crisis? What did emotional factors contribute? Some sense of what the crisis is and what caused it must be uncovered. If not, the wrong damage-containment mechanisms may be activated and give rise to other crises.

COMMUNICATION

The organization's CM team (CMT) must be notified and assembled as quickly as possible at the first sign of a crisis. This statement presupposes that team members can be located twenty-four hours a day, 365 days a year, and that every member has a permanent backup or replacement. It is also assumed that other key stakeholders (board members, federal regulators, outside crisis experts) can and will be contacted.

Among internal stakeholders, it is a good idea to have a single CMT facilitator and a single organizational spokesperson (not necessarily the same person). The CMT facilitator can act as the "point person" in collecting and disseminating CM information and in taking responsibility for CM decisions. The main job of the spokesperson is to communicate effectively to key internal and external stakeholders, in straightforward language. The use of technical jargon, excuses ("We didn't plan for this, because its probability of occurring was only one chance in a million"), or "No comment" may be interpreted as defensiveness or corporate arrogance. Because a key characteristic of crises is uncertainty, however, it is perfectly appropriate for the spokesperson to acknowledge that facts are not yet available, as long as a promise is made to convey additional information as soon as the facts are known. Indeed, the credibility of the spokesperson outweighs knowing *all* the facts or the truth in the heat of any major crisis; audiences accept that all the desired information is rarely available at the onset of a crisis.

WORST-CASE SCENARIOS

By definition, a worst-case scenario involves the occurrence of the least likely, least planned-for, least prepared-for events at the worst possible time and in the worst possible location. Thus, with respect to the variable of crisis types, a worst-case scenario involves the occurrence of at least one crisis that the organization is least prepared for or has discounted. The worst possible worst-case scenario involves the occurrence of a chain of unanticipated crises before or after a major crisis occurs. In other words, a worst-case scenario inevitably involves crises that the organization has not thought of or has discounted. In a worst-case scenario, the organization's crisis preparations (if any) actually contribute to the crisis.

With respect to crisis phases, a worst-case scenario involves an organization's failure to pick up early-warning signals of an impending crisis. It may even involve the blocking of signals or creation of faulty early-warning systems that give false readings or illusions of protection. Any worst-case scenario may also involve faulty preparation or prevention, ineffective damage containment, unsuccessful business recovery, and nonexistent learning mechanisms.

With respect to the variable of systems, a worst-case scenario involves faulty analyses of how core technology may fail or not fail. Risk analyses that assume ideal conditions lead to overconfidence and mispreparation. A worst-case scenario generally reflects a discounting of the role that human factors play in the creation of any major crisis. The same is true with respect to the organizational infrastructure: a major crisis occurs in a remote, inaccessible place at 6:00 P.M. on Friday or during the weekend, when critical personnel cannot be reached. Crucial communication lines break down, and a worst-case scenario exposes weaknesses in the organization's culture.

With respect to stakeholders, a worst-case scenario seems to prove the most damaging allegations of one's enemies: "The organization knew about the crisis but deliberately did nothing." A worst-case scenario also involves harm to the most vulnerable and innocent stakeholders: the unborn, children, the elderly, the infirm, and wildlife, including endangered species.

THE ABCO WORST-CASE SCENARIO

Let us return to the ABCO case, introduced in Chapter One. In addition to ABCO's failure to pick up early-warning signals of the crisis, a worst-case scenario might include an intentional coverup by ABCO's senior executives. Suppose that key senior personnel bribed officials to falsify water tests or to squelch inflammatory information about ABCO plant's operations. Suppose that employees were also intimidated into keeping quiet about their misgivings. In short, suppose that signals were not only denied but also intentionally blocked by ABCO's top management. (Perhaps ABCO's top executives even became arrogant enough to believe their own lies.)

There were no efforts to prevent an impending crisis—indeed, ABCO responded to news of it with arrogance, defensiveness, and denial of all wrongdoing. Evidence would confirm not only lack of investment in technological safeguards but also a trail of decisions in favor of short-term savings at the expense of safety. ABCO might have purchased substandard equipment or might knowingly have violated state or federal regulations. The company might be guilty of ignoring near-accidents, sharply declining morale, or poor safety records. In the most dramatic worst-case scenario, money thus saved would be found in senior executives' pockets. The culture could be characterized as silenced, with communication channels blocked both within and outside the organization. Creative energy would be invested in denying rather than preparing for a crisis.

In a worst-case scenario, there would also be a chain reaction of subsequent crises. At some point, ABCO could expect to experience a major crisis of confidence: employees would jump ship, former consumers would disparage ABCO's reputation, other members of the meat-packing industry would set off a backlash against ABCO, and the Middleton community would impede ABCO's progress at every possible junction. If the most damaging allegations of ABCO's enemies proved true, ABCO would find no support among its former allies.

BEST-CASE SCENARIOS

In a best-case scenario, the organization is prepared for the occurrence of at least one type of crisis in each of the crisis families. CM plans have been devised, and CM procedures have been practiced. Key stakeholders are knowledgeable and confident about the CM roles that they must fill. In fact, preparation includes planned redundancy, so that the possible absence of critical stakeholders has been foreseen, and alternates are ready to step in. There is a mindset of preparedness that permeates the organization: employees are informed about their CM responsibilities, and resources have been set aside for major contingencies.

The organization has mechanisms specifically tailored to detect, record, and disseminate signals of impending crises. Messengers of potentially bad news are not only tolerated but also encouraged to come forth; indeed, they are formally rewarded for reporting potential problems. Damage-containment elements have been tested and include backup facilities, supplies, and emergency response personnel. The organization has identified the resources needed for recovery of essential business services, and the contacts for securing those resources have been established. Information from previous crises and near-crises has been incorporated into organizational CM systems. The result of this learning is continual improvement of support technologies, enhanced matching between human-factors needs and capabilities, and a core culture that supports the sharing of resources and information. In a best-case scenario, all these strengths come together to enhance the organization's ability to manage a crisis.

THE ABCO BEST-CASE SCENARIO

Suppose, that ABCO was well prepared to manage the crisis. Instead of encountering an ill-equipped and out-of-date plant, we would find a plant where investment in maintenance, technology, and human factors exceeded minimal standards and needs. We would find a plant with an exemplary record of safety—a model plant, with minimum negative turnover and maximum precautions against occupational accidents. ABCO would be open to information about its crisis vulnerability, both from employees and from external auditors. In fact, ABCO would hire outside auditors to make continual assessments. When news of the crisis reached ABCO, executives would respond in a nondefensive, down-to-earth manner. The culture of the organization would reflect openness and honesty. And because this picture would do nothing to confirm the allegations of its enemies, ABCO's allies would remain loyal. Employees would keep their faith in ABCO, despite any provocative media coverage. Consumers would find reassurance in ABCO's long-standing reputation. Other members of the meat-packing industry would stand ready to support ABCO with public confirmation and resources. The Middleton community would support ABCO's decisions. Fully integrated crisis-preparedness would help ABCO manage the crisis and improve prospects of support from those outside ABCO.

PUTTING IT ALL TOGETHER

Exhibit 9.1 offers a systematic way to consider all the issues we have just discussed. The columns represent the various types of crises. Ideally, your organization will be prepared for at least one crisis from each family (refer also to Figure 2.2). For every individual crisis, see whether your organization's CM plans spell out what it will do across every row in the matrix. For instance, are there early-warning signal-detection mechanisms specified for use? As before, we suggest that you and your colleagues consider these elements together and discuss your responses to the questions found in Exhibit 9.2.

EXHIBIT 9.1.   **An Interactive Crisis Framework.**

	External Economic Attacks	External Information Attacks	Breaks	Psycho-pathology	Mega-damage	Occupa-tional Factors	Perceptual Damage	Human Resources
Phases Early warning Prevention Damage containment Recovery Learning								
Systems Core technology Organization Infrastructure Human factors Organization Culture Emotions								
Stakeholders Internal External								

SOURCE: *Crisis Management,* by Ian I. Mitroff and Christine M. Pearson. San Francisco: Jossey-Bass Publishers, © 1993. Permission to reproduce and distribute material (with copyright notice visible) is hereby granted. If material is to be used in a for-profit compilation, please contact publisher for permission.

EXHIBIT 9.2.   **Questions for Managing During a Crisis.**

---

1. How well prepared is your organization to assess immediate human casualties (deaths, injuries) and other damage during the first hours and days of a major crisis?

   a. What are the barriers to immediate asessment?

   b. Which individuals inside your organization have been assigned to assess immediate damage?

   c. How well trained are they?

   d. How easy are they to contact? to get to the site of the crisis?

2. How quickly can the members of your CMT be contacted and assembled?

   a. Is there a permanent twenty-four-hour, 365-day site or CMT control center or command room?

   b. Is the site sealed off, protected, and well staffed?

3. Who is responsible for analyzing causes of crises?

   a. Is contact information readily available? Is it on a computer? What happens if your computers go down? Can you still get the needed information?

   b. Can the persons responsible be located and assembled easily and readily?

   c. Do they know their roles? Have they practiced their roles under realistically simulated conditions?

4. How does your organization facilitate the analysis of the following major causes of crises?

- Technology?

- Organizational infrastructure?

- Human factors?

- Organizational culture?

- Emotions?

5. Who is responsible for damage control in the following areas:

- Technical?

- Legal?

- Political?

- Social?

- Psychological?

- Economic?

6. How quickly can you assess the state of your organization's damage-control mechanisms?

- How quickly can they be put into operation?

- Is medical help readily available? Psychological-trauma help?

7. Which key stakeholders need to be contacted or involved personally, by mail or other means?

   a. Internal (List with contact information.)

   - Medical personnel

   - Security personnel

   - Management personnel

   - Employees

   - Families

   b. External (List with contact information.)

   - Regulatory agencies

   - Competitors

   - Suppliers

   - Key customers

   - Others

8. Who is responsible for business-resumption plans and activities?

   - Stakeholders

   - Personnel at backup sites

   - Key customers

   - Suppliers

9. What are the key assumptions that underlie your CM response capabilities?

- Who knows the full set of assumptions?

- Who is responsible for testing them?

- What is the organization prepared to do if its key assumptions are no longer valid? (List major contingency and backup plans and actions.)

Chapter *10* The Components of
an Ideal CM Program

Because of the importance we attach to systemic, integrated, or what we have called *critical* thinking, we want to emphasize once again the components of an ideal CM program founded on what the best companies are doing. In particular, we want to discuss in more detail each of the elements (see Exhibit 10.1) presented in Chapter Two by taking you through examples of actual CM practices.

. . . .

STRATEGIC ACTIONS

As a general rule, current CM efforts are weak and fragmented. We have found that many of the Fortune 1000 companies have no plans for CM and that many have not created formal crisis management teams (CMTs). Among more than two hundred companies in which we have conducted interviews, we have also found that only 5 to 15 percent, at best, can be considered as having developed systemic strategies or approaches to CM. Only this small sample has implemented actions that cut across all five categories listed in Exhibit 10.1.

This chapter is based on Thierry C. Pauchant and Ian I. Mitroff, *Transforming the Crisis-Prone Organization* (Jossey-Bass, 1992).

EXHIBIT 10.1.   **Factors in an Ideal CM Effort.**

Strategic actions
- Drastic changes in corporate philosophy
- Integration of CM in mission statements and notions of corporate excellence
- Integration of CM in strategic planning
- Inclusion of outsiders on board and CM unit team
- Training and workshops in CM
- Crisis simulations
- Diversification and portfolio strategies

Technical and structural actions
- Creation of a CM unit team
- Creation of dedicated budget for CM
- Continually developing and changing emergency policies and manuals
- Computerized inventories of plants' employees, products, and capabilities
- Creation of a strategic emergency room or facilities
- Reduction of hazardous products, services, and production processes
- Improved overall design and safety of products and production
- Technological redundancy (such as computer backup)
- Use of outside experts and services in CM

Evaluation and diagnostic actions
- Legal and financial audit of threats and liabilities
- Modifications in insurance coverage
- Environmental-impact audits
- Ranking of most critical activities necessary for daily operations
- Early-warning signal detection, scanning, issues management
- Dedicated research on potential hidden dangers
- Critical follow-up of past crises

Communication actions
- Media training for CM
- Major efforts in public relations
- Increased information to local communities
- Increased relationships with intervening stakeholders groups (police, media)
- Increased collaboration or lobbying among stakeholders
- Use of new communication technologies and channels

EXHIBIT 10.1.	**Factors in an Ideal CM Effort.** *(continued)*

Psychological and cultural actions
  Strong top management commitment to CM
  Increased relationships with activist groups
  Improved acceptance of whistleblowers
  Increased knowledge of criminal behavior
  Increased visibility of the human and emotional impacts of crises
  Psychological support to employees
  Stress management and management of anxiety
  Symbolic recall and corporate memory of past crises and dangers

What fundamentally distinguishes crisis-prepared from crisis-prone organizations is their overall and integrated view of CM. Crisis-prepared organizations do not consider CM a cost of doing business; rather, they view it as a strategic necessity that provides a number of competitive advantages. This drastic shift in corporate outlook or philosophy is perhaps one of the most difficult and yet necessary tasks for an organization that wants to be prepared for a diverse set of crises. It means that executives in crisis-prepared organizations consider their firms not only as productive systems but also as potentially destructive systems. Executives in such firms debate issues that pertain to success, leadership, growth, and excellence, but they also consider and debate issues surrounding potential failure, breakdowns, decay, and death. They have developed the ability to imagine the worst, the unthinkable, the unspeakable, as a way of doing everything possible to prevent such events. Contrary to the conventional wisdom, crises do not "just happen" (especially humanly or organizationally induced crises).

This shift in corporate philosophy has a major impact on definitions of corporate excellence. One executive in the chemicals industry put the matter this way: "We not only have the responsibility to bring to our customers the best products possible at a competitive price, we also need to protect them from their products' most dangerous attributes or consequences." Crisis-prepared organizations have made substantial changes in the nature of their products and manufacturing processes, as a way of adhering to this new and expanded view of corporate excellence. For example, Johnson & Johnson has abandoned capsule forms of Tylenol. Others in the food and pharmaceuticals industries have developed antitampering packaging. Some chemicals firms have stopped manufacturing aerosol products, given their damage to the ozone layer. Some have developed a new "generation" of safer chemicals.

Integrating CM into the definition of corporate excellence is vitally important. When such integration is absent, many of the faulty beliefs that restrict or narrow definitions of corporate excellence become powerful barriers to the development of effective CM programs. Consider the remarks of one executive: "A formal program is not necessary for an excellent company. Our track record is so good that crises are not considered as a major risk for us. Only bad companies need crisis management to cover up their deficiencies." This executive has twisted the concept of excellence into an excuse for not developing an effective program of CM, and this sentiment is not atypical. But mistaken notions of excellence hardly render organizations immune to crises. Crisis-prepared organizations have come to understand that mistaken concepts of excellence, pushed to the extreme, may actually exacerbate crises: overconfident organizations tend not to prepare for the worst.

Crisis-prepared organizations have also integrated CM into strategic planning processes. Executives in such organizations emphasize that, like other issues, CM must involve top management if it is to be taken seriously. Since CM may involve the very survival of the whole operation, it must be considered explicitly by top management. The processes of crisis planning and learning are sometimes more important than the plans themselves (as is also true of issues involved in corporate strategy). As a result, executives in crisis-prepared organizations have come to see and use CM as a new tool for deriving competitive advantage. During one crisis, a bank operated a mobile unit for business areas affected by a power outage, thus allowing its customers to process their transactions without interruption. An executive of the bank said, "The crisis gave us the opportunity to really extend our services to our smaller clients. We started with the question 'What can hurt us?' and more recently changed it to 'What can hurt our customers?' "

As a way of challenging basic assumptions concerning corporate philosophy, notions of excellence, and strategy, some firms make a point of including outsiders in the formulation of crisis plans and procedures.

One firm in the chemicals industry has two environmental activists on its board. Another in the oil industry hires key executives with no previous background in the industry or its technology. Still other firms hire outside consultants as "insultants" (a term coined by Peter Drucker). A number of firms have instituted formal training workshops in CM, which extend far beyond traditional security issues. Others have initiated formal crisis simulations. Some firms take simulations seriously enough to use professional actors to play the roles of the media, government officials, and even terrorists. Diversification is widely used and accepted in such areas as finance and corporate strategy, but crisis-prepared organizations diversify in another way as well: they implement at least one action from each of the five categories listed in Exhibit 10.1. The notion of diversifying preparation for crises is considered vital to the crisis "portfolio."

TECHNICAL AND STRUCTURAL ACTIONS

The typical firm starts a program of CM either by reacting to a particular crisis or by focusing on a specific technical area. As an executive in the insurance industry explained, "It doesn't take great insight to realize that a bomb can be placed in your computer system."

One of the first tasks of the crisis-prepared organization is the formation of a crisis management team (CMT). At first, the primary function of the CMT is to provide a centralized power structure that can make and implement decisions rapidly in the midst of a crisis. CMTs are increasingly used outside crisis situations, however. In these cases, their function is to organize CM efforts that are more proactive in nature. They attempt to diminish the likelihood of crises and to develop organizational learning processes with regard to CM. In this form, they often assemble executives from various departments. Some firms complement this structure with more formal CM structures. Several corporations have vice presidents for crisis management, or for safety, health, and the environment. A CMT's effectiveness is enhanced by a dedicated budget for CM, the development of emergency manuals and policies, the creation of a computerized CM inventory system, and the creation of specific emergency facilities, which all signal the importance of CM in the organization.

Some firms also decentralize their decision making, so that they can take quick action in times of crisis. In an insurance company, for example, managers of operations were given full authority to "declare a disaster" and switch the operation of their information systems to an external firm specializing in computer emergencies.

Manuals created by crisis-prepared organizations are user-friendly and are continually updated under the supervision of the CMT. Some firms supplement their manuals with computerized data bases containing inventories of the supplies and resources that would be helpful in a major crisis. Some have even developed computerized decision aids for CM. One large manufacturer, for example, is building a computerized data base for each of its plants, which includes key contacts, the location of private communication channels, general plant history, names of employees, lists of potential hazards, detailed product inventories, emergency capabilities at sites and in the community, types of various health treatments to be administered for various types of emergencies, the historical track record of a plant's incidents and improvements, and the nature of the contacts with (and history of relationships with) local emergency services and government officials.

In some organizations, CMTs are assisted by the creation of dedicated emergency facilities similar to the "war rooms" developed by the military. One airline has built two of these facilities in strategic locations, equipped with the most advanced information systems and communication technologies.

Finally, other technical actions concern the reduction of hazards, the overall improvement of safety procedures, technological backup and redundancy in systems, and the use of outside experts in CM. We have already seen the importance of reducing hazards, in our discussion of changes in concepts of corporate excellence. Overall improvements in safety procedures regroup the tasks traditionally performed by security and safety personnel (screening employees, controlling restricted access to sensitive areas, improving inspection and quality-control procedures, using security groups, restricting access to computer facilities). But crisis-prepared organizations do not merely protect their existing products, services, and processes; they constantly reevaluate the need for redesign and modification.

· ·

EVALUATIVE AND DIAGNOSTIC ACTIONS

The third group of CM actions includes a number of diagnostic tools and evaluation processes. Some already exist in many organizations: legal and financial audits of threats and liabilities; modifications in insurance coverage; environmental-impact audits; and ranking of the activities necessary for daily operations according to how important they are.

Legal and financial assessment of threats and liabilities is standard procedure in corporations, but crisis-prone organizations often focus on these two areas alone. In such organizations, lawyers are most often the first to be contacted in a crisis, even before the ambulances are called. Such organizations often underrate the need to contain the threat itself.

Modification of insurance coverage is also a common strategy used in CM, but a number of issues fuel intense debate. These include the precise evaluation of insurance costs and coverage for environmental disasters, and the specific responsibilities of insurance companies if crises develop over time (as in cases involving asbestos). What seems to distinguish crisis-prone from crisis-prepared organizations is that the former often confuse insurance with CM itself. This position betrays two simplistic assumptions: that CM is solely reactive, to be used only after the occurrence of a disaster, and that CM is only a cost. This position ignores CM's competitive advantage.

Where environmental-impact audits are concerned, here again the crisis-prepared organization differs greatly from the crisis-prone one. Crisis-prepared organizations do not consider such audits a nuisance; they view them as opportunities to broaden the horizons of corporate excellence.

Many organizations explicitly rank their activities with respect to importance in daily operations. This assessment is different for every organization and depends on the nature of specific activities and on continuous reevaluation by the CMT. Some organizations assess the maximum number of days they can sustain daily activities without personnel, cash, technology, inventories, or data. Others determine the customers (stakeholders) or markets that they absolutely must serve. Still others rank the importance of their products and services.

Firms that have developed early-warning signal detection understand that most crises and disasters have a history that can inform current and future CM directions. For example, more than two dozen spills similar to but larger than the Exxon *Valdez* disaster took place outside U.S. waters prior to it. The *Challenger* disaster was preceded by a trail of memos that explicitly warned of danger. In some organizations, a professional staff scans examples of crises in the industry or in related areas. In others, this activity is included in existing programs for issues management. In still others, a director of communication networks assists the chief information officer in tracking specific issues. In all effective CM efforts, findings from such scanning activities are communicated directly to the CMT and are used to direct further CM activities.

A few firms have conducted research on potential hidden dangers in products, services, and production facilities and processes. These firms go beyond traditional strategic analysis of vulnerabilities, to focus on competitive moves, market fluctuations, regulatory changes, and innovations in technology. One large pharmaceuticals company has an "internal assassin" team, which attempts to tamper with and sabotage the company's products and manufacturing processes (see page 46). The same firm also has a "counterassassin" team, whose role is to protect products and facilities. A company in the insurance industry determined the "dependence costs" of its technologies, including total costs that might be incurred by the organization if its technologies failed. The company then refused to purchase a multimillion-dollar information system because too much dependence on the system constituted a competitive disadvantage.

One of the most difficult tasks of CM is to challenge the "invisibility of technologies"—to systematically expose and manage the dangers associated with their hidden aspects. The dangers are often only revealed through a crisis itself. After the Hinsdale outage, in which a fire in a suburban Chicago communications hub cut off telephone and computer service to thousands of subscribers for days and even weeks, executives and managers reported having gleaned a basic insight: they rediscovered the importance of the telephone. Firms that had not considered the danger of relying on telephone technology had focused their CM efforts on a limited and traditional set of security features. They backed up their records, protected access to their computers and computer facilities, and enhanced their own networks, without considering the total context: the telephone network.

Opportunities for learning from past crises are often taken only when an investigation is mandated by court order (such as in the *Challenger* disaster). Refusal to reflect on past disasters is understandable: the emotional burdens of major crises are extremely heavy. Nearly one-third of people involved in crises show symptoms of anxiety for three to five years afterward. But crisis-prepared organizations understand that crises can provide tremendous opportunities for learning and for enhancing future efforts.

COMMUNICATION ACTIONS

The fourth group of actions concerns how organizations manage communication and the kinds of information transmitted to and from stakeholders. Media training and efforts in public relations (PR) are very popular, and many consulting firms offer expertise in these areas. The media strategies used by Johnson & Johnson during the Tylenol crisis—high visibility, congruence, honesty, and caring—are seen as the model to be followed. Indeed, according to one PR director, crisis-prone organizations believe that "a good message can resolve a bad crisis." Crisis-prepared organizations recognize that unless PR is integrated with other actions, it may backfire and cause an even worse crisis. Crisis-prone organizations are often overconcerned with their public images, and they confuse the content of their messages with the reality of their crises. For example, an executive in a chemicals company defined a crisis for his organization as "being in the headlines." A public relations director in a gas company defined his job as "making our product invisible." This strategy is understandable, but it increases public ignorance of potential dangers. It goes directly against the grain of uncovering hidden dangers. (The residents of Bhopal believed that Union Carbide was producing a "plant medicine.")

Divulging information to local communities, such information about the nature of dangerous products, potential hazards, and emergency plans is another important action implemented by some organizations. (It is required by law in several industries.) In crisis-prepared organizations, dissemination of information is often coupled with an increase in relationships with police, health specialists, laboratories, emergency services, fire departments, and governmental agencies. Such groups are informed of potential hazards, and emergency plans are developed conjointly. Some organizations also develop strong relationships with local media representatives before a crisis, informing them regularly of improvements and changes in products, processes, and plants.

Crisis-prepared organizations collaborate much more frequently with other stakeholders, such as firms in the same industry, governmental agencies, suppliers, customers, and community members. Crisis-prepared organizations understand that secrecy is detrimental to effective CM. They recognize that they cannot manage major crises alone.

Crisis-prepared organizations also use different communication technologies and channels for crisis situations. In the United States, for example, some firms have created a network of 800-number emergency lines. Through them, the locations of calls received can be tracked instantaneously, to establish an ongoing geographical map of a crisis. Crisis-prone organizations tend to focus their efforts exclusively on communications among members of the organization and on technical data (accounting, inventory, or financial and marketing data). Crisis-prepared organizations focus on both internal and external communications, giving equal emphasis to technical and human communication. They acknowledge the paramount need to protect their technical data, but these firms also stress the need to protect and develop their voice communications—the human side of communication.

PSYCHOLOGICAL AND CULTURAL ACTIONS

Top management's strong commitment to CM sometimes entails a drastic shift in organizational values. We have found that the single most important factor in convincing senior executives of the need for CM is direct experience of a repeated series of crises. But the development of a systemic approach to CM also requires a fundamental shift in corporate philosophy—an understanding of the fact that a corporation may become destructive if critical issues are not addressed. CM requires the moral and political courage, as well as the cognitive and emotional strength, to face and discuss disturbing, uncertain, and anxiety-provoking issues.

Some companies have increased their relationships with activist groups. A firm in the telecommunications industry has developed a network of such groups, including minority groups, consumer groups, and social activists. This firm regularly polls these groups, to understand their views on crucial issues and report these findings to its CMT. Other firms have integrated representatives of activist groups into formal structures. What distinguishes crisis-prepared organizations is that these firms have avoided an "us versus them" mentality. They attempt to understand and integrate different perspectives.

Some crisis-prepared organizations systematically reward whistleblowers. Such organizations have developed an internal culture where the discussion of bad news is not only tolerated but also encouraged. In these companies, such discussion is so important that it is formally recorded in employee evaluations and even used in making promotion decisions. Other firms have initiated various bonus programs for employees and managers who uncover hidden dangers, malfunctions, or product defects.

A few firms have acted to increase their knowledge and understanding of criminal behavior. One company in the chemicals industry sponsors seminars for its managers on such subjects as the social and psychological roots of sabotage, the diagnosis of psychopathology in organizations, and the dynamics of terrorism, hiring experts in psychiatry, psychopathology, and criminal behavior. Unfortunately, because these subjects are not found in the basic curricula of business or engineering schools, most managers still lack basic training in tracking and handling complex behavior.

Some crisis-prepared organizations have increased the visibility of the human impacts of crises. For example, plant employees in an aerospace firm were briefed by a pilot who experienced a technical breakdown, which almost caused him to crash while testing a new airplane. The notion of quality control became less abstract, and the employees became more aware of their personal responsibility for the lives of others.

The experience of a disaster has serious psychological consequences. To manage the trauma often associated with a major crisis, some firms hire psychotherapists. NASA opened a crisis hotline for its employees after the *Challenger* disaster. Corporations increasingly are using the services of the postcrisis intervention teams of psychotherapists, social workers, and physicians that have been created in various communities to cope with the effects of natural disasters.

Stress management and anxiety management are more concerned with preparing managers and employees to function relatively well during a crisis and helping them uncover threatening issues on a day-to-day basis. Some firms focus their efforts on the members of the CMT. In conditions of severe stress, strong cognitive and affective biases may hinder decision making. Through workshops and crisis simulations, crisis-prepared organizations continually work on such biases, in order to lessen their impact.

Some firms also attempt to manage the anxiety that surrounds CM in general. This area is perhaps the single most difficult aspect of CM to address. Crisis-prone organizations use a number of defense mechanisms and faulty beliefs to rationalize why they do not need to put more emphasis on CM. Such defense mechanisms as denial, projection, and idealization of "saviors" are normal and healthy responses to major threats. They allow individuals to act in the face of terrifying problems. Carried to an extreme, however, such mechanisms also increase vulnerability by blocking individuals or organizations from evaluating or anticipating potential dangers. Crisis-prepared organizations understand this fundamental difference; their executives and managers allow themselves to be somewhat anxious.

Crisis-prepared organizations also understand that to formally acknowledge past crises is healthier than denying them. Even without formal acknowledgment, managers and employees remember crises anyway. Managers in one large organization wear black armbands to symbolize mourning on the anniversary of their most devastating crisis. Other companies have institutionalized mourning ceremonies and developed symbols of crisis events.

SUMMARY

We have not found a single organization that has developed all the CM strategies listed in Exhibit 10.1. But crisis-prepared organizations have made it an explicit policy to implement at least one of the strategies in each of the five groups listed. The list can be seen as the basis or cornerstone of an ideal CM strategic plan. It provides a basis against which you can compare the actions that have already been implemented in your organization.

Most current CM plans are dangerously fragmented, focusing primarily on one or two general areas. Technical actions are more developed in corporations than psychological and cultural CM strategies, and fewer than one-fifth of scientific articles on CM strategies even mention the psychological domain. But crisis-prepared organizations understand better that CM requires both technical and human actions.

Some of the strategies described in this chapter may seem somewhat anomalous in a business setting, but we believe that they will eventually become standard procedures. The purpose of CM is not exclusively to get back as soon as possible to "business as usual." At its core, CM requires the corporation to realize its moral and social responsibility to internal stakeholders, external stakeholders, society, and even the global environment. Crisis-prepared organizations have begun to integrate this responsibility into their corporate philosophy and business strategies. By doing so, they have also gained many advantages over their competitors. We believe that strategies being developed by these organizations will be some of the most important criteria for characterizing an "excellent" company in the twenty-first century.

Appendix

Current CM Practices Among the Fortune 1000 Companies

esearch at the University of Southern California (USC) Center for Crisis Management is concerned with understanding crises that are the result of human action or inaction and providing useful guidelines for those who are faced with these challenges as part of their job responsibilities. Surprisingly, in spite of the devastating effects that can be caused by crises, our early research indicates that most organizations do not have systematic, integrated means of managing them. We have also found the management literature to be virtually devoid of empirically based research on CM programs and strategies. To increase the level of understanding about CM as it is actually practiced in organizations across the country, the USC Center for Crisis Management distributed a questionnaire to Fortune 1000 executives during the spring and winter of 1990. The results of this research provide a basis to evaluate how your company is performing by comparison.

Our objectives in gathering this information were to ascertain (1) the current status of CM programs in America's largest companies, (2) CM executives' views of the optimal framework for CM efforts, (3) an understanding of the roles played by those responsible for CM, and (4) the characteristics of those organizations that have established a priority for CM. This appendix reflects the shared perspectives of the respondents, who represent the uppermost levels of the Fortune 1000 companies.

To capture the broadest range of CM strategies, we sampled the manufacturing and service sectors equally. Manufacturing was represented by publishers; firms in the food, chemicals, mining, oil, pharmaceuticals, petroleum, forest products, motor vehicle, building materials, metals, and electronics industries; and firms in computers, office equipment, textiles, transportation equipment, aerospace, soaps and cosmetics, furniture, and beverages. Service industries reflected in this research include financial institutions, utilities, life insurance, transportation, retailing, and diversified services.

TYPES: MISMATCHED THREATS AND OPPORTUNITIES

We asked the respondents to assess their CM vulnerabilities. For most executives, the greatest imaginable threat strikes closest to the heart or core of their organizations' business. Chemicals companies worry most about toxic leaks. Banks are most concerned about plunging financial reputations. In the manufacturing industries, accidents, technical breaks, product tampering, and natural disasters are most threatening. The service industries include these disasters but add economic and information attacks, as well as such human violations as kidnapping and assaults on customers. Overall, those organizations that produce tangible products worry about production and distribution. Those that create intangible services worry about the loss of reputation and information.

Executives indicate confidence in their organizations' ability to dealing with technical breaks or physical damage. Arenas of crisis-preparedness are generally localized (for example, accidents confined within a factory or facility). Respondents believe that if a crisis is contained, the organization will be capable of managing it. But one of the most amazing (and perhaps most alarming) findings of this study is that nearly half of the respondents believe that their organizations are not equipped to handle the crisis that they specifically identify as the most threatening. There is a mismatch between the crises they prepare for and the crises that most threaten them. The following responses typify this dissonance: between crisis vulnerability and crisis preparation.

Greatest threat	*Threat best prepared for*
Nuclear accidents at power plants	Union strikes or financial troubles
One of our employees going crazy and killing people	Computer failure
Loss of skilled personnel	Fire, windstorm
Kidnap and ransoming of executives	Physical damage to plant
Product liability	Robbery, fire
Environmental accident	Computer or MIS failure

The high incidence of this disjunction suggests the CM preparations of many organizations are not matched to their vulnerabilities.

PHASES: STILL CAUGHT IN THE HEAT OF CRISIS

Most of the Fortune 1000 organizations have detailed plans for containment of specific disasters (such as fires or product tampering), but fewer than half have plans for business resumption. Still fewer have any means of formally integrating CM lessons that they have learned. Fewer than 25 percent have any systematic signal-detection mechanisms in place. In general, organizations tend to pour resources into activities that take place in the heat of a crisis.

SYSTEMS: MINDSET VERSUS PRACTICE

We asked respondents to describe the current state of their organizations' CM practices. Most report that top management believes that the company is vulnerable to crises, and nearly all respondents feel that top management now acknowledges the need for CM. Indeed, 90 percent believe that their organizations can afford to spend time and money on things that might happen to them. In short, organizational mindset supports CM. But this group also describes a number of shortcomings in current CM programs. They indicate that top executives acknowledge the need for CM, but they also describe an ambivalent attitude among senior managers and local (site) field managers, which inhibits progress in CM practice. Top executives may recognize the value of CM, but operating managers are not yet committed. Some respondents also report that their CM efforts are curtailed by a disjointed, disorganized approach, because centralized, corporatewide systems do not exist. For some, attempts to push CM efforts to lower levels have been fully derailed. In these organizations, while CM values may already have taken root in the most senior management ranks, they have not found favorable "growing conditions" throughout the organization.

While the vast majority of respondents believe that knowledge of CM procedures should filter throughout the organization, CM support systems are not in place. Some companies have no written CM plans. In many that do have plans, the plans are out of date or address only a limited array of crises or have not been tested in drills, simulations, or actual crises. Respondents also characterized their CM systems as weak because of communication breakdowns, including the inability of the CM to function as a team, especially if the CEO is absent for any reason.

In spite of these weaknesses, more than half of the executives believe that their companies can handle any problem that may occur. Since most also report that their CM programs are in the early stages of development, this view may reflect overconfidence in current CM capabilities, as well as oversight or denial of current vulnerabilities. Nevertheless, although they are still building their programs, they do describe the strengths of their CM systems, especially senior executives' support for CM efforts and overall cultural flexibility. Three-quarters of the respondents feel that the time and energy invested in CM make their business operations more effective. Senior management supports CM in the majority of these organizations by participating on CM teams. According to the respondents, top management's participation guarantees that a CMT will be highly experienced and knowledgeable. High-level CMTs also have the authority to implement key decisions and quickly attain essential resources. Cultural flexibility in support of CM is characterized as effective communication (from the top down, from the bottom up, and across the organization) and as the ability to quickly adapt organizational strategies to shifting priorities in the event of a crisis.

STAKEHOLDERS: CM TEAMS

To learn more about optimal CM planning, we asked participants to share their opinions about what the best CM programs should include. More than 90 percent of the respondents believe that top executives should oversee crisis management; but for CM programs to succeed, they feel that representation in making CM decisions must be shared with middle management. In fact, 80 percent of the executives surveyed believe that CM should not take place at the top levels only; in their view, knowledge of CM procedures should be filtered to employees at all levels of the organization. Nearly 75 percent of these leaders suggest that, in the ideal case, even line workers should be represented on CM teams. The majority of respondents also believe that CM should not be a separate function reporting directly to the CEO, but that employees at all levels should be held formally accountable for crisis management responsibilities. In terms of the actual state of crisis management programs in the Fortune 1000 sample, nearly 75 percent of the organizations have CM teams (CMTs) that comprise representatives from various levels of the organization.

To evaluate CMT capabilities, we asked which functions tended to be represented on the teams and which tended to dominate CM decisions and activities. Management information systems (MIS) and public relations (PR) directors dominate CM decisions, followed closely by security and legal functions. Our respondents report that in their organizations the main influence on CM operations is least likely to come from finance or human resources (HR) directors. Dominant roles vary, but most of those surveyed indicate that their CM teams include representatives of all these functions (MIS, PR, security, legal, finance, and HR), plus marketing and quality assurance).

WHERE DO WE GO FROM HERE?

Organizations that recognize the need for CM tend to equip themselves with more CM tools and techniques (CMTs, early-warning tracking systems, business-resumption plans, emotional support services). Once they have recognized the need for CM, they are willing to dedicate the time and money necessary to put CM programs in place. This effort may include introducing CM plans for all levels of the organization or extending the CMT beyond the senior executive ranks. To fortify CM values, organizations that include middle managers and line workers on CMTs also attach responsibility to those rights: employees are formally held accountable for implementing CM efforts.

As the magnitude and the impact of human-induced crises continue to expand, most organizations will need to close the gap between desired and achieved levels of crisis-preparedness. Many need to take a step back, to reassessing the match between their greatest threats and their CM capabilities. In the selection of which crises to prepare for, familiar crises and strategies are too often favored. As a result, organizations may miss or even avoid opportunities to reduce their risks by addressing less familiar crises. What makes this gap even more disconcerting is that the respondents themselves estimate that the crises for which they deem themselves underprepared would cost hundreds of millions of dollars.

Many envision implementing CM throughout their entire organizations, but CM efforts still lag. In most organizations, additional actions must be taken to disseminate CM to all levels and functions. Middle-level and line employees, who are often in the best position to perceive or contain a crisis, must be prepared. It is equally important that CM plans and procedures move beyond containing a crisis once it hits. To curtail crises in the incipient stages, organizations that value CM can begin to incorporate effective early-warning signal detection. The earlier an organization detects an impending crisis, the more it can do to head the crisis off. We urge leaders to share their CM experiences and learning, so that we can all do more to prevent major crises.

Complete prevention of crises is impossible, of course, but many human-induced crises are preventable in principle. Organizations that do not try to prevent them may find such crises compounded by loss of reputation. Doing everything humanly possible to curtail crises is a realistic goal for all organizations.

Bibliography

Bowonder, B., and Linstone, H. A. "Notes on the Bhopal Accident: Risk Analysis and Multiple Perspectives." *Technological Forecasting and Social Change,* 1987, *32,* 183–202.

Dutton, J. E. "The Processing of Crisis and Non-crisis Strategic Issues." *Journal of Management Studies,* 1986, *23,* 501–517.

Fink, S. *Crisis Management: Planning for the Inevitable.* New York: AMACOM, 1986.

Fink, S., Beak, J., and Taddeo, K. "Organizational Crisis and Change." *Journal of Applied Behavioral Science,* 1971, *7,* 15–37.

Gephart, R. P., Steier, L., and Lawrence, T. "Cultural Rationalities in Crisis Sensemaking: A Study of a Public Inquiry into a Major Industrial Accident." *Industrial Crisis Quarterly,* 1989, *4,* 27–48.

Lagadec, P. "Communication Strategies in Crisis Situations." *Industrial Crisis Quarterly,* 1987, *1,* 19–26.

Lagadec, P. "Principles and Checklist for Handling Postaccident Crises." Paper presented at the Second International Conference on Industrial and Organizational Crisis Management, New York University, Nov. 1989.

Meyers, G. C. *When It Hits the Fan: Managing the Nine Crises of Business.* New York: New American Library, 1986.

Mitroff, I. I. *Break-Away Thinking: How to Challenge Your Business Assumptions (and Why You Should).* New York: Wiley, 1988.

Mitroff, I. I., and Kilmann, R. H. *Corporate Tragedies: Product Tampering, Sabotage, and Other Catastrophes.* New York: Praeger, 1984.

Mitroff, I. I., and Pauchant, T. C. *We're So Big and Powerful That Nothing Bad Can Happen to Us.* New York: Carol Publishing, 1990.

Mitroff, I. I., Pauchant, T. C., and Shrivastava, P. "Conceptual and Empirical Issues in the Development of a General Theory of Crisis Management." *Technological Forecasting and Social Change,* 1988, *33,* 83–107.

Mitroff, I. I., Pauchant, T. C., and Shrivastava, P. "Forming a Crisis Portfolio." *Security Management,* 1988, *33,* 101–108.

Nystrom, P. C., and Starbuck, W. H. "To Avoid Organizational Crises, Unlearn." *Organizational Dynamics,* 1984, *12,* 53–65.

O'Connor, J. *The Meaning of Crisis: A Theoretical Introduction.* Oxford: Basil Blackwell, 1987.

Schwartz, H. S. "Organizational Disaster and Organizational Decay: The Case of the National Aeronautics and Space Administration." *Industrial Crisis Quarterly,* 1989, *3,* 319–334.

Schwartz, H. S. *Narcissistic Process and Corporate Decay: The Theory of Organization Ideal.* New York: New York University Press, 1990.

Sehti, S. P. "The Inhuman Error: Lessons from Bhopal." *New Management,* 1985, *3,* 40–44.

Shaw, L., and Sichel, H. S. *Accident-Proneness: Research in the Occurrence, Causation, and Prevention of Road Accidents.* Elmsford, N.Y.: Pergamon Press, 1971.

Shrivastava, P. *Bhopal: Anatomy of a Crisis.* New York: Ballinger, 1987.

Slaikeu, K. A. *Crisis Intervention. A Handbook for Practice and Research.* Boston: Allyn & Bacon, 1984.

Smart, C. F., and Vertinsky, I. "Designs for Crisis Decision Units." *Administrative Science Quarterly,* 1977, *22,* 640–657.

Smart, C. F., and Vertinsky, I. "Strategy and the Environment: A Study of Corporate Responses to Crises." *Strategic Management Journal,* 1984, *5,* 199–213.

Pauchant, T. C., and Mitroff, I. I. "Crisis Prone Versus Crisis Avoiding Organizations." *Industrial Crisis Quarterly,* 1988, *2,* 53–63.

Pauchant, T. C., and Mitroff, I. I. "Crisis Management: Managing Paradox in a Chaotic World—The Case of Bhopal." *Technological Forecasting and Social Change,* 1990, *38,* 99–114.

Pauchant, T. C., Mitroff, I. I., and Pearson, C. "Crisis Management and Strategic Management: Similarities, Differences and Challenges." In P. Shrivastava, A. Huff, and J. Dutton (eds.), *Advances in Strategic Management.* Vol. 8. Greenwich, Conn.: JAI Press, 1991.

Pauchant, T. C., Mitroff, I. I., Weldon, D. N., and Ventolo, G. F. "The Ever Expanding Scope of Industrial Crises: A Systemic Study of the Hinsdale Telecommunications Outage." *Industrial Crisis Quarterly,* 1990, *4,* 243–261.

Perrow, C. *Normal Accidents: Living with High-Risk Technologies.* New York: Basic Books, 1984.

Reilly, A. H. "Are Organizations Ready for Crisis? A Managerial Scoreboard." *Columbia Journal of World Business,* 1987, *22,* 79–88.

Report of the Presidential Commission on the Space Shuttle Challenger *Accident.* No. 04000000496-3. Washington, D.C.: Government Printing Office, 1986.

Rushdie, S. *The Satanic Verses.* New York: Viking-Penguin, 1988.

Sobel, R. *Panic on Wall Street.* New York: Dutton, 1988.

Starbuck, W. H., and Milliken, F. J. "*Challenger:* Fine-Tuning the Odds Until Something Breaks." *Journal of Management Studies,* 1988, *25,* 319–340.

Weick, K. E. "Organizational Culture as a Source of High Reliability." *California Management Review,* 1987, *24,* 112–127.

Weir, D. *The Bhopal Syndrome: Pesticides, Environment and Health.* San Francisco: Sierra Club Books, 1987.

Wildavski, A. *Searching for Safety.* New Brunswick, N.J.: Transaction, 1988.

Wilkinson, C. B. "Aftermath of a Disaster: The Collapse of the Hyatt Regency Hotel Skywalk." *American Journal of Psychiatry,* 1983, *140,* 1134–1139.

Index